AF786376

FSC
www.fsc.org
MIX
Papier aus verantwortungsvollen Quellen
Paper from responsible sources
FSC® C105338

Vincent Schade

Successful Management of Mergers & Acquisitions

Development of a Synergy Tracking Tool for the Post Merger Integration

Anchor Academic
Publishing

Schade, Vincent: Successful Management of Mergers & Acquisitions. «Untertitel», Hamburg, Anchor Academic Publishing 2013

Buch-ISBN: 978-3-95489-165-8
PDF-eBook-ISBN: 978-3-95489-665-3
Druck/Herstellung: Anchor Academic Publishing, Hamburg, 2013

Bibliografische Information der Deutschen Nationalbibliothek:
Die Deutsche Nationalbibliothek verzeichnet diese Publikation in der Deutschen Nationalbibliografie; detaillierte bibliografische Daten sind im Internet über http://dnb.d-nb.de abrufbar.

All rights reserved. This publication may not be reproduced, stored in a retrieval system or transmitted, in any form or by any means, electronic, mechanical, photocopying, recording or otherwise, without the prior permission of the publishers.

Das Werk einschließlich aller seiner Teile ist urheberrechtlich geschützt. Jede Verwertung außerhalb der Grenzen des Urheberrechtsgesetzes ist ohne Zustimmung des Verlages unzulässig und strafbar. Dies gilt insbesondere für Vervielfältigungen, Übersetzungen, Mikroverfilmungen und die Einspeicherung und Bearbeitung in elektronischen Systemen.

Die Wiedergabe von Gebrauchsnamen, Handelsnamen, Warenbezeichnungen usw. in diesem Werk berechtigt auch ohne besondere Kennzeichnung nicht zu der Annahme, dass solche Namen im Sinne der Warenzeichen- und Markenschutz-Gesetzgebung als frei zu betrachten wären und daher von jedermann benutzt werden dürften.

Die Informationen in diesem Werk wurden mit Sorgfalt erarbeitet. Dennoch können Fehler nicht vollständig ausgeschlossen werden und der Diplomica Verlag, die Autoren oder Übersetzer übernehmen keine juristische Verantwortung oder irgendeine Haftung für evtl. verbliebene fehlerhafte Angaben und deren Folgen.

Alle Rechte vorbehalten

© Anchor Academic Publishing, Imprint der Diplomica Verlag GmbH
Hermannstal 119k, 22119 Hamburg
http://www.diplomica-verlag.de, Hamburg 2013
Printed in Germany

Table of Contents

Table of Figures

List of Abbreviations

CAPM	Capital Asset Pricing Model
DCF	Discounted Cash Flow
DD	Due Diligence
KPI	Key Performance Indicator
IT	Information Technology
LoI	Letter of Intent
M&A	Mergers & Acquisitions
NDA	Non-Disclosure Agreement
NPV	Net Present Value
PMI	Post Merger Integration
PV	Present Value
TV	Terminal Value
WACC	Weighted Average Cost of Capital

1 Introduction

1.1 Background & Purpose

In Business Development, Mergers & Acquisitions (M&A) have become an increasingly attractive growth opportunity among companies over a long period of time. Nowadays, there is hardly a day where current developments of ongoing M&A transactions or speculations about presumed M&A deals cannot be followed in the daily press. Other external growth opportunities, such as strategic alliances, joint ventures, and franchising (inorganic growth) are still behind M&A as a strategic alternative. Organic growth, which can be achieved by increasing sales personnel, developing new products or expanding in new geographical areas, presents another alternative. Nonetheless, M&A are often preferred because they provide a faster way to enter new markets and to make operations more efficient.[1] Moreover, the constantly increasing global competition, strengthened through lowered market entry barriers and trade enhancing conventions between several countries, contribute to an increased consolidation pressure among businesses.[2]

However, it turned out that M&A are fairly sensitive projects that are vulnerable to fail. It is proved that a huge number of M&A did not deliver on their promises.[3] The majority of failed M&A are a result of mismanagement during the Post Merger Integration (PMI) when processes have to be adjusted, personnel need to be teamed up and corporate cultures have to be reconciled.[4] The importance of the PMI within M&A transactions was determined during a survey among leading managers by the consulting firm AT Kearney (See Figure 1):

[1] See Coenenberg; Jakoby 2000, P.178.
[2] See Lucks; Meckl 2002, P.6-7.
[3] See Booz Allen & Hamilton 2001.
[4] See Gerds; Schewe 2009, P.4-6.

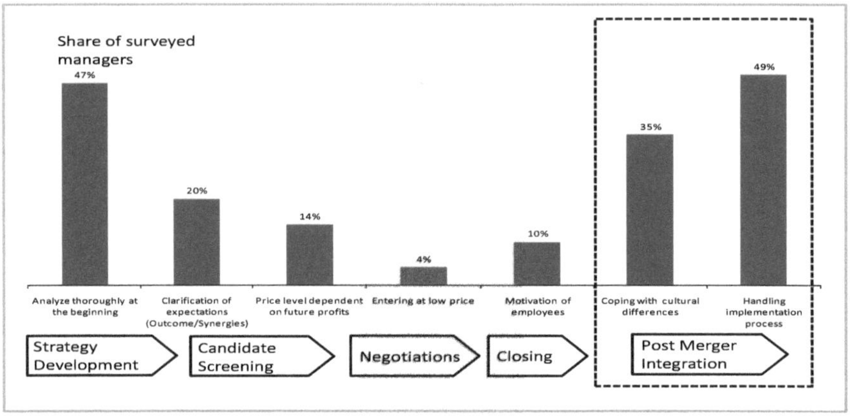

Source: Own illustraion based on A.T. Kearney Global PMI Study 2002/2003

Figure 1: Critical Factors of Success in Mergers and Acquisitions

During the PMI, synergies, as the dominant motive for M&A, which are identified before the transaction, have to be realized.[5] However, synergies can frequently not be realized due to a poor quality of information, a high level of complexity or bad implementation strategies.[6] In spite of these difficulties, many companies have not established a well-functioning synergy management and synergy tracking in their organizational structures yet.[7]

This study deals predominantly with aspects of synergy management whereby the main focus is on synergy tracking as a support function of the synergy management. An emphasis is on the analysis of realization efforts that need to be done by the management during the PMI. To provide a solution and ease the aforementioned issues of synergy realization, a synergy tracking tool, which serves as an effective support instrument during the PMI is developed.

1.2 Methodology

The introductory part of this study is followed by the theoretical framework that comprises chapter two and three. In the second chapter, fundamentals and principles of M&A science are analyzed in order to provide the reader with necessary background knowledge in topics of M&A. It follows an introduction of synergies, as the value driver in M&A, in chapter three. In addition, different types of synergy potentials in M&A transactions are defined and synergy

[5] See Unger 2007, P.880.
[6] See Deloitte 2009, P.8.
[7] See Thomaschewski 2004, P.117.

risks are discussed. The body of this study includes the three subsequent chapters. In Chapter four the general necessity of synergy management and synergy tracking within M&A is explained and a distinction between these functions is made. Furthermore, the tasks of synergy tracking are described in detail and challenges which have to be coped with while synergy tracking are addressed. In order to provide a comprehensive understanding of the synergy tracking tool, the valuation of synergy potentials is the main topic in chapter five. In this context the Discounted Cash-Flow analysis (DCF), as the dominant method of company valuation as well as the valuation of synergy potentials, is discussed. The synergy tracking tool is presented in chapter six. After the description of the structure, certain features required to fulfill the tracking tasks are explained. The study ends with a summary of the main aspects of synergy management and future perspectives for the M&A market.

2 Mergers & Acquisitions

2.1 Definition and Distinction of Mergers & Acquisitions

The term M&A, which refers to Mergers & Acquisitions, comes originally from the Anglo-Saxon language and has not been commonly defined yet. Overall, it includes all processes that deal with the sale or the purchase of companies or parts of companies whereas the change of the ownership structure is considered as the main characteristic.[8]

An acquisition is defined as a purchase of a company, a part of a company, majority- or minority ownership. A merger on the other hand is a consolidation of two or more independent companies whereby at least one part loses its autonomy.[9] Hence, M&A have to be differentiated from strategic cooperations, such as joint ventures and strategic alliances that are characterized by contracts between the parties involved.[10] In addition, cooperation agreements are time-limited while M&A are rather considered to be long-lasting.[11] However, this distinction is called into question since the activity of financial investors that aim for quick profits by investing in companies, such as Private Equity firms, has increased on the M&A market.

Several criteria are used to classify M&A transactions. In the following, the criteria are chosen based on their particular impact on synergies in M&A.

2.2 Selected Types of Mergers & Acquisitions

2.2.1 Strategic Alignment Approach

M&A transactions can be divided into horizontal, vertical, and conglomerate M&A. A horizontal M&A refers to a transaction which takes place between companies within the same industry that operate on the same value-added step.[12] A popular example for a horizontal M&A transaction is the merger between the auto manufacturer Daimler and Chrysler in the year 1998. The main motives of these M&A transactions are often to increase market share, to improve the competitiveness by acquiring direct competitors or realize cost synergies, such as economies of scale and scope.[13] Companies involved in a vertical M&A also share the same industry, but operate on different steps of the value chain. Motives for this type of M&A are often to extend the vertical integration within the value chain or to discard dependences on supplier or customer.[14] As last type within the strategic alignment approach, conglomerate M&A are to be addressed. These are transactions which take place between entities that do

[8] See Lucks; Meckl 2002, P.23.
[9] See Coenenberg; Jakoby 2000, P.178.
[10] See Jansen 2001, P.110.
[11] See Paprottka 1996, P.8.
[12] See Fischer 2008, P.18.
[13] See Wirtz 2003, P.18.
[14] See Paprottka 1996, P.11-12.

not compete on the same market. Conglomerate M&A provide businesses with the option to have instant access to new markets. Companies engaged in this type of M&A transaction search for new business opportunities on new markets or try to lower their operational risk by diversification.[15]

2.2.2 Attitude Approach

Most of this study assumes that the target company is interested in the buyer`s offer and is a willing participant in the acquisition process (friendly takeover). However, a considerable portion of M&A transactions are events in which not only the ownership structure is affected, but also the management of the target company is replaced and changes in leadership style and business strategies are enforced by the acquirer. Therefore, resistance on the side of the target company can often be experienced. The management tries to avert the M&A approach for instance by implementing "poisen pills"[16] or by encouraging other companies to enter a bid competition in order to force up the deal value. These so called hostile or unfriendly take-overs cause often particular difficulties in the synergy management process since important information about the acquisition target are not provided and have to be gathered from public sources.[17]

2.2.3 Regional Approach

M&A have become increasingly international during the last years. This increase is a result of major economic forces which have been pushed forward, such as the European Union's single market, the globalization of the marketplace and the increasing global competition. Many companies realized that they need to go global in order to maintain a competitive edge. This development has resulted in a significant increase of cross-border M&A over the last years.[18] However, cross-border M&A compared to domestic M&A are particularly exposed by the risk of failure. This has mainly to do with the high degree of complexity that has to be dealt with when M&A are conducted and synergies are due to be created. Companies involved in these transactions have to manage issues, such as cultural differences, different business laws, and varying market regulations.[19] Therefore, international M&A projects need to be carefully planned and systematically conducted to a particular extent.[20]

---

[15] See Wirtz 2003, P.19.
[16] See DePamphilis 2009, P.106.
[17] See Weber; Roventa 2006, P.281.
[18] See Lucks; Meckl 2002, P.3-5.
[19] See Fischer 2008, P.20-21.
[20] See Lucks; Meckl 2002, P.252-267.

2.3 The M&A Process

Generally it can be said that M&A transactions fulfill all characteristics of a project, which are the uniqueness of the goal, time limitation, complexity, shortage of resources, and strategic importance.[21] M&A transactions are complex projects in which many different parties and people are involved and need to contribute in order to achieve the proposed outcome. Therefore, most M&A transactions follow a similar pattern and go through a typical series of actions.[22] According to most scientific literature this process is divided into three main phases, even though there are also sources that follow a multi-phase model.[23] In the following, the M&A process is described based on the three phase model from the acquiring company`s point of view (See Figure 2):

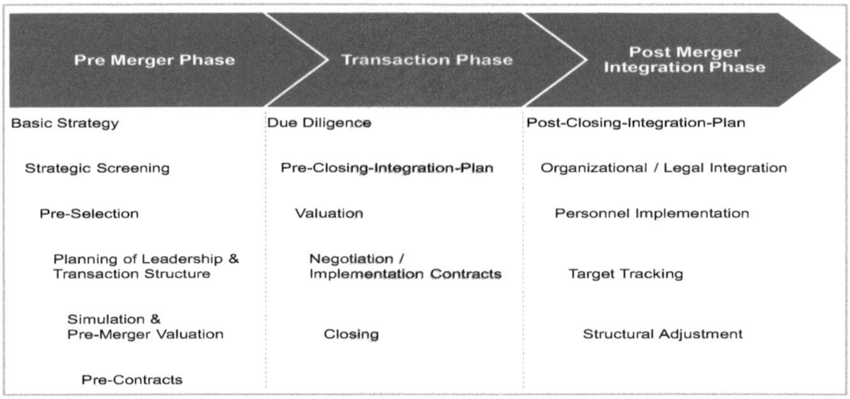

Source: Own illustration based on Lucks; Meckl 2002, P. 54.

Figure 2: The M&A Process

Selected actions are described that have to be taken during the respective phases to ensure a successful M&A transaction and to give an overview over the main tasks during an M&A process. A complete and detailed analysis of all steps that are shown on the graph cannot be provided in this study. Hence, the description is limited on the core content of the actions shown on the chart.

[21] See Sodeik 2009, P.47.
[22] See Fischer 2008, P.34-35.
[23] See Gerds 2000, P.12.

2.3.1 The Pre Merger Phase

During the pre merger phase the basic strategy has to be determined and strategic goals need to be defined. At the same time, other alternatives, such as internal growth strategies are to be analyzed and compared with the proposed M&A strategy. This is fundamental to decide whether external growth creates the most value for the company and should be done before every M&A proposal.[24]

After the decision for an M&A was made and the management defined common strategic goals, the acquirer searches for the ideal partner to accomplish the strategic objectives. Before the management conducts the strategic screening for possible candidates, it creates a company profile which incorporates all required characteristics that the target company has to possess. The so-called Long List includes all interesting companies that might be approached. These companies are later evaluated by means of their strategic, cultural, and financial fit to the acquiring company, which then leads to a more comprised list (Short List). The strategic screening of potential M&A partner prevents integration since fundamental problems emerging later in the M&A process can be foreseen.[25]

The first contact to the selected companies takes place during the pre-selection process. At this stage, the potential target companies are approached in order to assess their willingness of an M&A transaction. Moreover, further information about the potential acquisition targets is gathered and used as additional selection criteria.[26]

Within the planning phase, the management has to agree on the legal form of the new organization and need to decide how the target company is to integrate in the organizational structure. In addition, the general transaction structure, if asset or share deal, and its financing have to be clarified.[27] Moreover, responsibilities for the further M&A process have to be assigned and decision power among these people has to be determined.[28]

An initial company analysis is done during the simulation phase. The future developments of the company on stand-alone basis as well as of the combined companies after the merger are evaluated. This analysis helps to identify actions that are required to optimize the M&A process. In addition, synergy potentials are initially analyzed so that the management can obtain a first overview of the possible advantages and negative effects in case of an M&A transaction.

A first estimation of the target company`s value is done during the pre-merger valuation phase. Although at this time only little information to calculate a reliable value of the target

---

[24] See Lucks; Meckl 2002, P.55, 74.
[25] See Fischer 2008, P.38; Lucks; Meckl 2002, P.79-86.
[26] See Lucks; Meckl 2002, P.87-88.
[27] Further reading about transaction structures provides: Wirtz 2003, P.257-258.
[28] See Lucks; Meckl 2002, P.97-107.

company is available, it gives an idea about the expected amount to invest. Thus, it helps when decisions about the financing of the transaction are to be made and enables to approach potential investors at an early stage.

Moreover, core areas that need to be particularly investigated during the Due Diligence can be de determined.[29]

At the end of the pre merger phase contracts, such as the Non-Disclosure Agreement (NDA) and the Letter of intent (LoI), have to be signed.[30] The NDA engages the contracting parties to treat all information which is provided during the M&A transaction confidentially and prevents misuse by third parties. A LoI is a non-binding summary about the general outlines of an M&A transaction and underlines the parties` interest in the M&A proposal. Therefore, conceptual issues, such as misinterpretations and other factors that can expose the M&A proposal in the ongoing process can be avoided on either side.[31]

2.3.2 The Transaction Phase

The transaction phase of the M&A process begins with the Due Diligence (DD) of the target company. The DD is a complex investigation of the target company`s current situation in which core aspects for the valuation of the acquisition target are analyzed to gain essential company information. Based on the results of the DD a realistic estimation of the target company`s value can be made. At this stage, the vendor provides the acquirer with all information that is required to evaluate the target company, thus the DD helps to estimate synergy potentials, which result from the merger, and to assess risks involved in the transaction. In addition, it helps the acquirer to derive a price range for negotiations about the final deal value.[32] A traditional DD incorporates three fields of investigation: financial, tax, and legal DD. However; this approach falls to short in ensuring a successful M&A transaction since it fails to consider potential issues during the PMI, such as "employee resistance". Therefore, aspects concerning human capital should also be part of the DD.[33] An in-depth DD significantly increases the likelihood of success in M&A, because it creates a foundation to identify synergy potentials.[34] The Due Diligence builds then the information source for the pre-closing-integration-plan. Moreover, actions required to realize synergy potentials are specified and part of in this plan. These actions have to be allocated to their respective departments to engage people with these tasks. Furthermore, the actions must be scheduled and milestones for integration projects of

[29] See Borowicz et al. 2006, P.169.
[30] See Ibid.; Picot 2008, P.159-162.
[31] See Bragg 2008, P.10-13, 83-85.
[32] See Picot 2008, P.166.
[33] See Deloitte 2009, P.12; Chapter 4.5.
[34] See Weber; Roventa 2006, P.281.

the PMI are to define. To ensure a manageable integration process and enable support functions like synergy tracking, synergy potentials have to be quantified.[35]

The actual valuation of the acquisition target takes place during the subsequent valuation phase. All knowledge about the acquisition target gained during the DD provides important input for this process, which can now be conducted based on a sufficient information basis. It has to be noted, that the result of this valuation represents only the so-called subjective value of the acquiring party's point of view and not the final deal value.[36] Essentially, it presents the maximum price which the acquirer would pay for the acquisition target.[37]

Several methods to value a company exist.[38] In this study the Discounted Cash Flow analysis (DCF) is applied as the most used method in practice.[39] The first step by valuing the acquisition target is to calculate the Stand-alone value which is the company value assumed that the acquisition target would continue to operate as it did before. Afterwards, restructuring potentials that would arise from an M&A transaction, such as the disposal of redundant asset and the estimated synergy value, are added.[40] Eventually, value decreasing effects, such as dysergies and integration costs have to be subtracted (See Figure 3):

[35] See Lucks; Meckl 2002, P.111-117; Chapter 4.2.
[36] See Lucks; Meckl 2002, P.175-176.
[37] See Wirtz 2003, P.202-203.
[38] See Lucks; Meckl 2002, P.177.
[39] See chapter 5.2 for a detailed analysis.
[40] Further reading relating the controversial discussion about the general distinction of restructuring potentials and synergy effects: See Metz 2002, P.60.

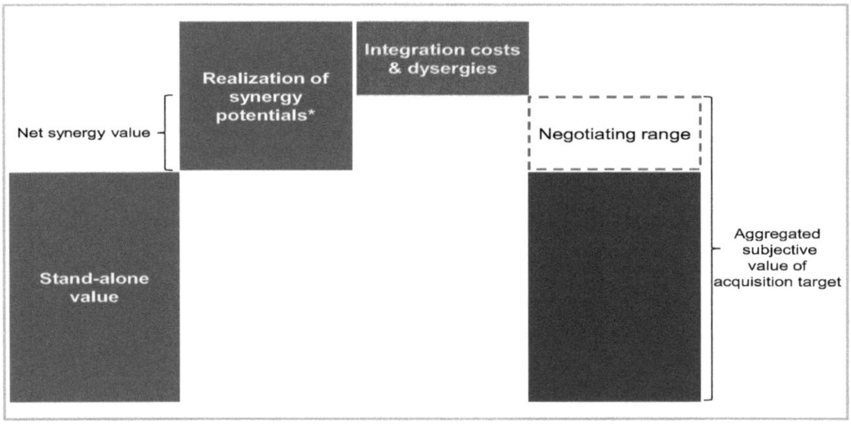

* Restructuring potentials included
Source: Own illustration based on Coenenberg; Jakoby 2000, P.196; Fischer 2008, P.57.

Figure 3: Step Model of Subjective Company Valuation

From the chart above, it can be concludeded that the final deal value is set within the negotiating range to an amount that both parties finally agree on. The exceeding amount of the Stand-alone value that has to be paid is called the price premium.[41] In order to add value through the M&A transaction, the Present Value (PV) of the net-synergy effects has to be higher than the price premium. Thus, it can be concluded that the identified synergies justify the price premium. [42] Likewise, it makes demands for the synergy management to realize synergies at least to the amount of the price premium to prevent value destruction after the transaction.[43]

The valuation is regularly done by both sides and results in different prices due to different objectives of the parties involved. In particular, differences concerning the valuation of restructuring potentials and synergy values can often be noticed.[44]

When both parties choose to continue with the M&A transaction after the valuation and potentials resulting from the merger are disclosed, they enter into the negotiation phase. The final deal value depends often on factors such as, market power, and negotiating skills of the parties involved[45]

After both parties agreed on a deal value, contracts must be signed as an official purchase agreement (Signing). In addition, implementation contracts that include additional agreements

[41] See Thomaschewski 2004, P.99.
[42] See Ibid.; Chapter 3.4.
[43] See Biberacher 2003, P.369-371.
[44] See Lucks; Meckl 2002, P.190.
[45] See Lucks; Meckl 2002, P.191; Wirtz 2003, P.256.

relating warranties and underwriting terms that were given by the parties during the process have to be signed.[46]

The transaction phase ends with the closing after approvals from public authorities, such as the Antitrust Division, were given.[47]

2.3.3 The Post Merger Integration Phase

The Post Merger Integration (PMI) has a huge impact on the success of M&A transactions.[48] In this phase previously planned synergies, which were calculated in the deal value, have to be realized in order to achieve the initial goals.[49] Although the PMI is often seen as the final phase of the M&A process, important tasks, such as personnel integration and target tracking, have to set in at earlier stages to ensure a successful integration process. Gerds & Schewe suggest a separate "Merger DD" to overcome risks, such as "employee resistance" and poor-quality information, which cause problems during the PMI.[50] Therefore, PMI is sometimes also seen as a cross-sectional phase of the M&A process.[51]

To make sure that all necessary actions are taken to meet the initial goals, a Post Merger Integration plan has to be created. In this plan the required tasks are timed and assigned to the persons in charge in order to keep the process manageable.[52] It builds on the pre-merger integration plan and can be seen as an extension of this under improved conditions and a higher level of detail.

During the organizational integration, all operations, which were earlier done separately, need to be combined.[53] The degree of integration and the pace in which the integration process is conducted are influential factors in this phase. Despite the pursuit of a short integration process in many businesses, problems caused by overloaded employees must be considered. Hence, it is important to adjust the pace of integration to the abilities of the workforce.[54] The legal integration as another task of the PMI refers to obligations, such as requesting the record in the company register for the newly formed business.[55]

During the personnel implementation, the management has often to deal with issues, such as job insecurity among employees and the refusal to adapt to new corporate cultures.[56] For this

[46] See Lucks; Meckl 2002, P.118-119.
[47] See Ibid.
[48] See Picot 2008, P.23.
[49] See Jansen 2001, P.227.
[50] See Gerds; Schewe 2009, P.122-130.
[51] See Jansen 2001, P.227.
[52] See Lucks; Meckl 2002, P.218.
[53] See Gerds 2000, P.51.
[54] See Deloitte 2009, P.17.
[55] See Lucks; Meckl 2002, P.129.
[56] See Larsson 2005, P.189-190; Chapter 4.5.

reason, it is necessary to incorporate incentive systems to keep employees motivated and to ease their apprehensions.[57]

Target tracking within the PMI comprises actions, such as synergy management and synergy tracking. The main task is to monitor business processes and make adjustments in order to realize synergy effects. At the same time, measures in respect of human capital such as, monitoring the development of the workforce to prevent losses of key employees are to be induced.[58]

Finally, structural adjustments due to the M&A transaction should be addressed in this context. These adjustments are required if it turns out that the integrated entity do not contribute to the firm`s strategy after all. These restructuring measures are often not done until a few years after the merger when it became evident that strategic goals cannot be achieved.[59]

---

[57] See Lucks; Meckl 2002, P.141.
[58] See Ibid., P.154, 220.
[59] See Ibid., P.130.

3 Synergies in Mergers & Acquisitions

3.1 Definitions and Distinctions of Synergy Terms

In order to avoid misinterpretation the term synergy which is often misinterpreted is defined in this chapter. In addition, a transition from the general term to synergies in the M&A context is made. The term synergy derives its origin from the word "synergo" which can be split into the two components "syn" (together) and ergo (work).[60] Discussions and debates about synergies in the business context often refer to Ansoff's synergy concept that he developed in contribution of science in corporate strategy. He describes positive synergies as the "2+2 = 5" effect which means that companies are able to add value while combining its product-market posture.[61] Nowadays, synergy is frequently used as a comprehensive term that embraces positive synergies and negative synergies which are also called dysergies.

Positive synergies in the business context are defined as "synchronic interactions of previously independent companies, subsidiaries or functional departments, which lead to an increase of the company value." Dysergies, on the contrary, are defined as "synchronic interactions of previously separated companies, subsidiaries or functional departments, which lead to a decrease of the company value."[62]

In the following, the term synergy is used comprehensively and refers to positive as well as negative synergies.

Another important distinction has to be made between the terms synergy effect and synergy potential. As synergy potential can be seen the economic effect which is expected when the separate entities are operating as one unit. Whereas the synergy effect describes the actual outcome after the synergy potential had been realized. This can be either a beneficial effect or a negative effect resulting from the M&A transaction. The following figure visualized these differences (See Figure 4):

---

[60] See Goold; Campbell 1998, P.133.
[61] See Ansoff 1965, P.72.
[62] See Biberacher 2003, P.53.

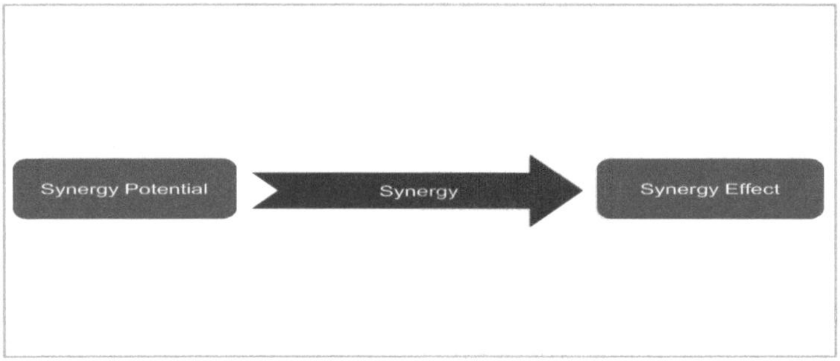

Source: Own illustration based on Thomaschewski 2004, P.16.

Figure 4: The Synergy Realization Process

3.2 Typical Synergy Potentials in Mergers & Acquisitions

Business science provides a variety of systematization methods for synergies.[63] In the following, synergies are categorized into functional, financial, and management synergies. This approach comprises the majority of synergy potentials and provides a structured overview.[64] It is paramount for the synergy management that synergy potentials are quantifiable; hence, Sirower describes synergies appropriately as "real, measurable improvements in competitive advantage."[65]

3.2.1 Functional specific Synergy Potentials

As functional specific synergy potentials can be described a synergy potential which can be precisely assigned to a certain functional department in an organization. Basically synergy potentials which are attained through an M&A transaction can be identified in every functional department of an organization, even though the myth that synergies exist only in back-office areas enjoys still popularity.[66] Indeed, it is not denied that synergy potentials in back-office areas, such as administration, accounting, and IT-departments can be obtained. However, most of them are entirely focused on cost reduction, such as job consolidation. Although, revenue-enhancing synergy potentials create often several alternatives to benefit from M&A.[67] As an example, an increase in revenues that results from cross-selling by the two firms after the merger. These cross-selling effects arise for instance when additional products

[63] See Ansoff 1965, P.75-76; Paprottka 1996, P.77-88; Beck 2003, P.676-680; Bruner 2004, P.327-332.
[64] See Thomaschewski 2004, P.17.
[65] See Bruner 2004, P.325.
[66] See Weber; Roventa 2006, P.281.
[67] See Bruner 2004, P.328.

from one company can be sold because of existing customer relations from the other company.[68] Further synergy potentials that can be assigned to this category are the economies of scale and economies of scope that are achieved in the production department. Economies of scale describe the effect when unit costs can be decreased due to an output increase which results in lower overhead costs per product.[69] Economies of scope on the other hand are cost reductions that are related to the product variety of companies. Cost savings may result from simultaneous production of several different products in a single business, as contrasted with their production in isolation, each by its own specialized firm. An example would be the platform production within the automobile industry where same parts can be used for assembling of different types of cars.[70] The following figure provides an overview of synergy potentials within the functional departments of an organization by combination of production factors (See Figure 5):

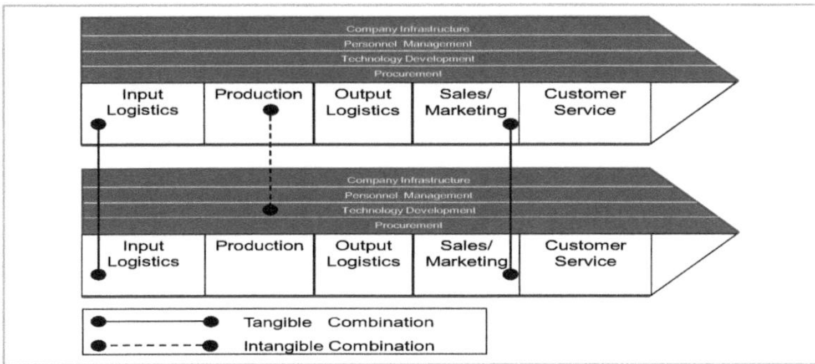

Source: Own illustration based on Porter 1999, P.421.

Figure 5: Synergy Potentials within the Value Chain

[68] See Fischer 2008, P.30; Another example provide: Lechner; Meyer 2003, P.368-369.
[69] See Jansen 2001, P.74-75; Deimel; Isemann; Müller 2006, P.69.
[70] See Jansen 2001, P.74.

3.2.2 Financial specific Synergy Potentials

In scientific literature financial synergies often play a minor part compared to the aforementioned synergy potentials. This is because they normally do not have to be realized under great effort as other synergies and do not cause comparable problems.[71] Mostly financial synergies are a consequence of the increase of the company size of the acquirer after the M&A transaction.[72] Yet, they can have a big impact on the acquiring business. Consequently, they need to be mentioned in this context. Financial synergies are distinct since they can result in two forms which are either higher cash flows or a lower the cost of capital.[73] A merger of two firms for instance results in a higher degree of creditworthiness when an emerging company which has credit constraints merges with a company with a high equity ratio and a high creditworthiness.[74] As a result, financing becomes cheaper and the cost of capital decreases. Another example would be the decrease of operational risk caused by non-perfectly correlated revenues of the involved companies. This can be the case when companies acquire complementary business segments after the merger. As a result the expected return on debt and equity decreases, and therefore the cost of capital (Co-insurance effect).[75] Also tax benefits as a special form of financial synergies belong to this category. These effects can arise either from the acquisition taking advantage of tax laws to write up the target company's assets or from the use of net operating losses to offset income. Thus, a profitable business which acquires a loss making firm may be able to use the net operating losses of the latter to ease its tax burden. Alternatively, a company that is able to increase its depreciation charges after an M&A transaction can save in taxes and shelter income (depreciation tax shield).[76]

3.2.3 Management specific Synergy Potentials

At this point the management synergy potentials as the last group of synergy potentials shall be addressed. Like the financial synergies, management synergies are able to have an impact on the entire acquiring company.[77] This can be achieved through the transfer of human capital. For instance managers with high potential and outstanding skills can be employed and bring positive effects into the newly-formed company. This can lead to an increase of productivity within the workforce as enhanced leadership style motivates employees and results in performance improvements. On the other hand, the number of highly-paid management posi-

[71] See Biberacher 2003, P.65.
[72] See Gildemeister 2008, P.20.
[73] See Damodaran 2005, P.4.
[74] See Beck 2003, P.679.
[75] See Wöginger 2004, P.206.
[76] See Biberacher 2003, P.65-67; Bruner 2004, P.328-329.
[77] See Thomaschewski 2004, P.17.

tions can often also be reduced which then leads to a decrease in labor costs.[78] Management synergy potentials can sometimes cause problems in particular when synergies are to be quantified in order to calculate the company value. Therefore, scoring models, such as the well-known balanced scorecard are often used to make qualitative synergies measurable.[79]

3.3 Synergy Pitfalls

M&A have been an established strategic option of business development for a long time. Consequently, managers of acquisitive businesses should have experience to manage these processes appropriately. Nonetheless, often they are not able to deliver synergies to the projected extent and do not achieve an M&A success. This can have several reasons. The three most mentioned synergy pitfalls are addressed in the following.[80] Synergy potentials tend to be overestimated. This is often the result of estimated synergy values by the management. Often manager fail to analyze synergy potentials in detail and do not consider their characteristics appropriately. Factors, such as the realization probability and the duration of synergies are often neglected.[81] Moreover, synergies are often planned top-down by the management which often leads to unrealistic assumptions that cannot be fulfilled by the people in charge.[82]. Another reason for a poor synergy realization effort is bad integration management. Common mistakes in this regard are insufficient project planning or an excessive pace of integration which can lead to dissatisfaction within the workforce and evoke employee resistance.[83] These dysergies and other integration costs are often neglected and hamper the synergy realization in eventual stages of the M&A process.[84]

3.4 The Connection between Synergies and the Price Premium in M&A

One of the most important tasks within M&A transactions is the valuation of the target company. The projected deal value of an M&A transaction is a crucial factor which determines whether external growth compared to other strategic options presents the most beneficial alternative in order to achieve strategic goals, such as the increase of the company value.[85]

In M&A transactions it has to be differentiated between the calculated company value and the final deal value. The reason for this deviation is because of the transaction partners and their

---

[78] See Beck 2003, P.679.
[79] See Reinke 1996, P.46-47.
[80] See Picot 2008, P.25; Beck 2003, P.680.
[81] See Unger 2005, P.887; Lechner; Meyer 2003, P.369-370.
[82] See Wöginger 2004, P.205; Weber; Roventa 2006, P.281.
[83] See Deloitte 2009; Gerds; Schewe 2009, P.70-88; Chapter 4.5.
[84] See Beck 2003, P.680.
[85] See Lucks; Meckl 2002, P.171-173.

different interests in the transaction. The vendor aims to get the maximum price for his/her company while the acquirer tries to achieve a price discount by applying risk surcharges and negotiating a low price premium to benefit from the transaction. Moreover, opinions about the allocation of synergies differ between the transaction parties. This means synergies are seen to be paid by the acquirer, whereby the acquirer expects to participate in their realization without paying for them. Regarding to this it is said that cost synergies, whose realization depends not on a particular acquirer (universal synergy effects), should generally be part of the price premium and should be paid by the acquirer. Whereas synergies, which can only be realized by a small group of companies, should only be calculated in the acquirer`s subjective value of the acquisition target and should thereby create a real synergy potential (real synergy effects).[86] Nevertheless, the final deal value is always an outcome of a market process in which different expectations are matched through price negotiations. Therefore factors, such as negotiation power and negotiation skills play a decisive role.[87] Generally, a common value in an M&A transaction does not exist since it always depends on which party of interest the respective value is calculated.[88]

In M&A Transactions, synergies are often the most influential value drivers. The synergy value has at least to cover the price premium in order to avoid value destruction.[89] The higher the price premium, the more synergies have to be realized by the acquirer in order to obtain a positive Net Present Value (NPV). Consequently, the acquirer`s economic break-even in which the risk-adjusted price premium is just compensated by the transaction can be determined as follows:[90]

Deal Value = Stand-alone value + Net synergy value

It should be noted, that the price premium equals the difference between the deal value and the Stand-alone value. Hence, the break-even formula can be simplified as:

Price premium = Net synergy value

Thus, it appears that a positive NPV can only be achieved when the net synergy effects exceed the price premium paid for the acquisition target. This highlights once more the importance of an effective synergy management during the entire M&A process and stresses the risks of value destructive M&A transactions as a result of overestimated synergy potentials.

[86] See Gildemeister 2008, P.60.
[87] See Thomaschewski 2004, P.97; Gildemeister 2008, P.59-60; Wala 2008, P.61; Eckhoff 2006, P.199.
[88] See Coenenberg; Jakoby 2000, P.185.
[89] See Lucks; Meckl 2002, P.186.
[90] See Thomaschewski 2004, P.99.

4 Synergy Management and Synergy Tracking in the M&A Process

4.1 Fundamentals of Synergy Management and Synergy Tracking

Synergies as described in the previous chapter are regularly dominant factors in deal values of M&A transactions. Often strategic decisions, such as increasing the company value through external growth, depend on attainable synergy potentials.[91] However, synergies are not realized by themselves. Hence, it is necessary to conduct an effective synergy management in order to achieve the defined goals.[92]

Synergy management within M&A projects has to overcome problems relating synergy realization which are often caused by complex implementation proposals by the top management or insufficient planning of synergy potentials in previous stages of the M&A transaction.[93] As earlier mentioned, it is often led by the top management via top-down decisions. However; it is increasingly recommended to integrate employees working in the departments where synergies have to be created.[94] The synergy management has three core elements which are the identification, quantification, and the ultimate realization of synergy potentials.[95] It is assisted by the synergy tracking which can be seen as a support function of the synergy management. Synergy tracking embraces two different types which depend on the issues to deal with. On the one hand the strategic synergy tracking which deals mainly with comprehensive topics, such as corporate environment, corporate structure and aspects of corporate culture. On the other hand the operational synergy tracking which is concerned with synergies that generally arise in the departments like cost synergies as a result of optimized business processes. In the following, the emphasis is on the operational synergy tracking where the majority of synergies need to be monitored.[96]

The requirements on synergy tracking are the same as those on the management control. Consequently synergy tracking has to gather, process, and provide information for the synergy management in order to support the decision-making process.[97] This implies that the synergy tracking ideally has to set in during the pre merger phase in order to meet its requirements.[98] The following chart illustrates tasks, integrated in a circular flow, that are imposed to the op-

---

91 See Coenenberg; Jakoby 2000, P.195.
92 See Weber; Roventa 2006, P.281.
93 See Lechner; Meyer 2005, P.14.
94 See Weber; Roventa 2006, P.281; Thomaschewski 2004, P.113.
95 See Biberacher 2003, P.96.
96 See Biberacher 2003, P.220, 349.
97 See Biberacher 2003, P.345; Deimel; Isemann; Müller 2006, P.24.
98 See Bire 2009, P.2.

erational synergy tracking in order to serve the synergy management appropriately (See Figure 6):

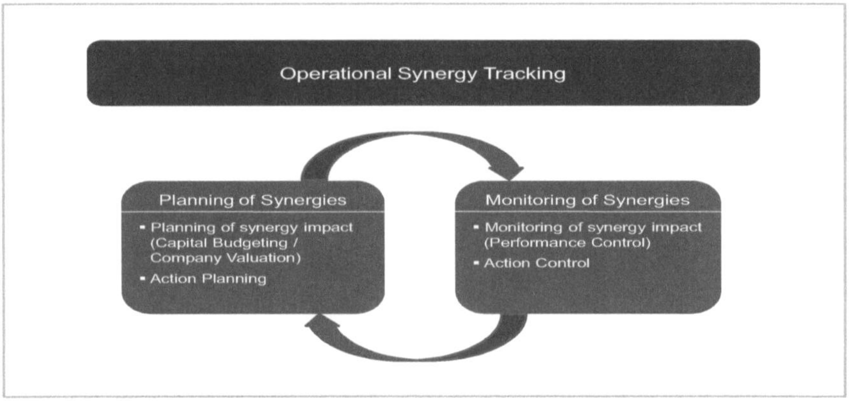

Source: Own illustration based on Biberacher 2006, P.293.

Figure 6: Systematization of Operational Synergy Tracking

As can be seen above, synergy tracking should be conducted as a cycle of actions in which synergy effects and the related actions are constantly monitored. When it appears that synergies are not realized as initially planned, adjustments have to be made which then lead to a modified planning. Moreover, synergy tracking supports the synergy management in identifying dysergies so that counter-measures can be initiated in time.[99]

[99] See Biberacher 2006, P.293.

The following step model illustrates the main tasks of the synergy tracking as a series of actions (See Figure 7):

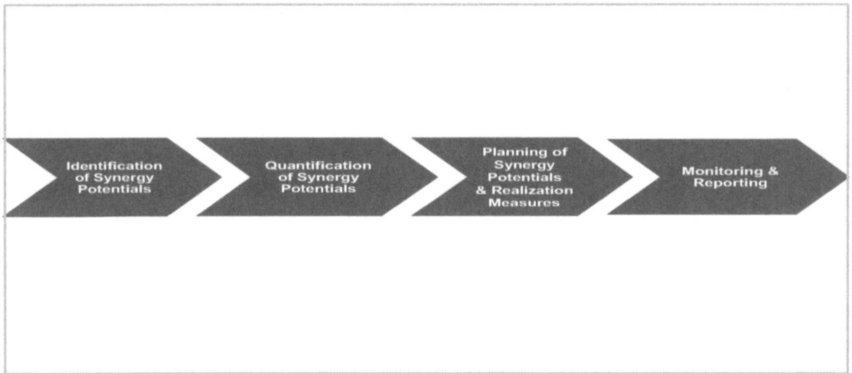

Source: Own illustration based on Beck 2003 , P.681.

Figure 7: Elements of Synergy Tracking

4.2 Requirements on Synergy Tracking during M&A Projects

4.2.1 Identification of Synergy Potentials

According to empirical studies and based on practical experiences, many M&A transactions fail due to a lack of realized synergies within the PMI. Analyses prove that one of the crucial mistakes is an insufficient planning of synergy potentials in previous stages of the M&A transaction. Often synergies are not systematically planned and quantified but merely managed at a high company level and estimated in a lump sum.[100]

In order to increase the company value through synergy realization an early planning of synergy potentials and their impact on financial figures is necessary.[101] During the Due Diligence in which confidential information about the target company is provided, an initial identification of synergy potentials should be conducted.[102]

M&A transactions offer regularly several opportunities to create synergies, such as business processes that can be combined after the M&A transaction. Therefore, not all areas in which operations can be optimized to gain positive synergy effects are instantly apparent. Weber & Roventa recommend setting up an exploration team consisting of selected managers from both companies to overcome this complexity issue and conduct knowledge transfer about

[100] See Unger 2007, P.887.
[101] See Biberacher 2006, P.293.
[102] See Borowicz et al. 2006, P.360-361; Weber; Roventa 2006, P.281.

company specific affairs.[103] Due to the variety of areas in which synergies can occur, a systematic synergy-scan should be implemented.[104] Hereby, the focus should not only be limited on the synergies themselves, but also on how synergies are achieved in the respective business areas to disclose and comprehend cause-effect relations.[105] Therefore, a synergy analysis cannot be exclusively focused on numbers but has to provide an overall view, thus synergy drivers can be identified. These are effects that directly impact on synergies resulting in the actual values expressed by financial figures.[106] As mentioned before, synergy tracking should also be focused on the identification of dysergies and integration costs. In many cases the underestimation and negligence of these effects causes M&A transactions to fail.[107] Hence, it is important to conduct an analysis in this respect and tackle these issues by identifying negative effects at an early stage and enable the synergy management to make realistic assumptions about the synergy value.

In addition, it is recommended to categorize synergies concerning their type in strategic, operational, and financial synergies. This gives the management a well-structured overview of the different synergy potentials. It also provides a picture about the realization efforts to spend, since often synergies of the same category share similar characteristics in terms of their risk profile of realization and their time of realization.[108]

4.2.2 Quantification of Synergy Potentials

It is often said:"You cannot control what you cannot measure." This implies that quantified synergies are a prerequisite to allow for a functional synergy tracking.

Synergy quantification also provides the synergy management a foundation for the post merger integration strategy. Business areas that offer large synergy potential or involve high integration costs become transparent so that synergy realization plans can be created.[109] This is of particular interest when synergies should be ranked by their priorities to generate so-called "early-wins". These are high-yielding synergy effects which potentially become beneficial in a short time without spending extensive effort and resources for their realization.[110]

Furthermore, M&A transactions are predominantly highly competitive bidding contests among several businesses which strive to increase their market share or to enter into new markets. This often results in excessive deal values because of exaggerated price premiums

---

[103] See Weber; Roventa 2006, P.282.
[104] See Weber; Roventa 2006, P.282.
[105] See Biberacher 2006, P.293.
[106] See Ibid.; Biberacher 2003, P.83-93.
[107] See Weber; Roventa 2006, P.280.
[108] See Bire 2009, P.2-3.
[109] See Bruner 2004, P.327.
[110] See Weber; Roventa 2006, P.284; Unger 2007, P.888-889.

which need to be paid to win the bid for the acquisition target.[111] These so-called strategic acquisitions are exposed by a high risk to fail since price premiums are not entirely covered by current synergy potentials.[112] This is an example which underlines the importance of synergy quantification as one of the main tasks of synergy tracking. The quantified synergies also provide the basis to calculate the possible price premium and the overall value, that are justified for the target company, before entering a bidding contest with other competitors.[113] For this reason, the synergy tracking is expected to express synergy potentials in an aggregated number reflecting the overall synergy value and quantify synergies in detail.[114] The latter is crucial to assign responsibilities to employees who are in charge of the respective departments in which the synergies are meant to be realized. Hence, it contributes to sustain a manageable process at the operational level.[115] However, in synergy tracking the principle of economic efficiency, which means cost-benefit aspects, should always be considered.[116] In this respect, implementation costs should be kept down by using the available information technology (IT)-systems and pre-existing tracking tools to operate an IT-based synergy tracking.[117] This also leads to consistent reporting tools in the company so that misinterpretations of reports can be prevented.[118]

Moreover, synergy tracking is regularly conducted under uncertainty. Synergies need to be planned and quantified before the actual realization takes place. This implies synergy tracking always has to consider risks involved in the realization of synergies while calculating the synergy values. Therefore, synergy tracking must be conducted carefully to prevent an overestimation of synergy potentials. In order to take risks into account during the calculation process, the synergy tracking uses techniques, such as scenario- and sensitivity analysis, in which value-added variables are modified in different scenarios, to examine their impact on the synergy value.[119] Furthermore, there are methods in which synergy realization risk is considered by applying risk-related discount rates in DCF analysis.[120]

Another difficulty which the synergy tracking faces while quantifying synergies is caused by the variety of qualitative synergies that often exist within M&A transactions. Qualitative synergies are effects that cannot simply converted into numbers to make them measurable like those that emerge by increasing customer satisfaction or a loss of reputation, as to mention a

---

[111] See Bire 2009, P.2.
[112] See Biberacher 2006, P.292.
[113] See Bire 2009, P.3.
[114] For a detailed analysis of the calculation process: See chapter 5.
[115] See Al-Ani; Rettberg; Humburg 2005, P.196.
[116] See Eckhoff 2006, P.72.
[117] See Ibid., P.72-73.; Thomaschewski 2004, P.116-117.
[118] See Weber; Roventa 2006, P.283-284; Eckhoff 2006, P.78-79.
[119] See Lucks; Meckl 2002, P.187.
[120] See Bruner 2004, P.332-333.

negative synergy effect. Discussions about the necessity to quantify those qualitative synergies are not indisputable because of their varying subjective importance of their respective assayer.[121] There are methods, such as scoring-models, that are applied to encounter this issue. However, this study is more concerned with quantitative synergies and does not provide a comprehensive analysis of different techniques to measure qualitative synergies.[122]

4.2.3 Planning of Synergy Potentials and Realization Measures

Apart from their quantification, synergies need to be planned relating their time, duration, and frequency of occurrence.

Synergies emerge at different times depending on their types. As an example, cost synergies, such as lower procurement costs due to increasing market power, can usually be obtained earlier than synergies that demand reorganization measures like decreasing production costs due to higher capacity utilization. Generally synergies should be realized once they arise so that a depreciation of their value caused by a higher discounting of their cash flows can be averted.[123] In addition, the dynamic business environment exposes a postponed synergy effort as well as other internal and external factors and can jeopardize synergy realization.[124]

Moreover, the dynamic business environment, that companies are affected by, influence the duration of synergies. Highly dynamic industries, such as the IT industry demand high flexible and innovative businesses. Product lifecycles are short so that new products need to be launched frequently on the market to keep pace with competitors. As a result, synergies emerging through know-how transfer or because of cross-selling effects cannot be declared as long-lasting and should be projected in a realistic forecast. This enables the synergy management to analyze synergy impacts over their time of existence and plan them appropriately.[125]

Furthermore, the frequency of occurrence of synergy effects has to be considered to ensure a precise calculation of synergy values. On the one hand there are nonrecurring synergies like integration costs. On the other hand financial synergies, such as lower interest expenses due to a permanent decrease in inventories, belong to the recurring synergies.[126]

Another task of synergy tracking at this stage is to determine measures that need to be carried out to realize the synergy effects and launch the respective projects.[127] Hence, an action plan, as an additional controlling instrument, should be set up which incorporates every project required to realize the projected synergy effects, the synergy potential, as well as the expected

[121] See Köppen 2004, P.124-125.
[122] An analysis of scoring-models provide: Biberacher 2003, P.124-130; Thomaschewski 2004, P.215-223.
[123] See Chapter 5.2 for further reading.
[124] See Eckhoff 2006, P.64-65.
[125] See Kerler 1999, P.26; Eckhoff 2006, P.65-66.
[126] See Thomaschewski 2004, P.25.
[127] See Biberacher 2006, P.293, Weber; Roventa 2006, P.284.

implementation costs calculated in the business plans. As a result, budgets to each project can be allocated in order to keep synergy-related expenses under control.[128] In addition, responsibilities have to be assigned to the synergy projects and significant stages of the projects, such as milestones are to be recorded.[129] This helps to trace resource constraints within the company so that priorities for the order of task fulfillment can be determined by the synergy management.[130]

In summary it can be said that the action plan serves as controlling tool in which actions are specified, valued, timed, and responsibilities are delegated among the workforce. Thus, it helps to make adjustments in case of variances and supports to recognize risks at an early stage in order to provide a sophisticated monitoring and reporting.[131] An exemplary action plan for synergy tracking is illustrated in the figure below (See Figure 8):

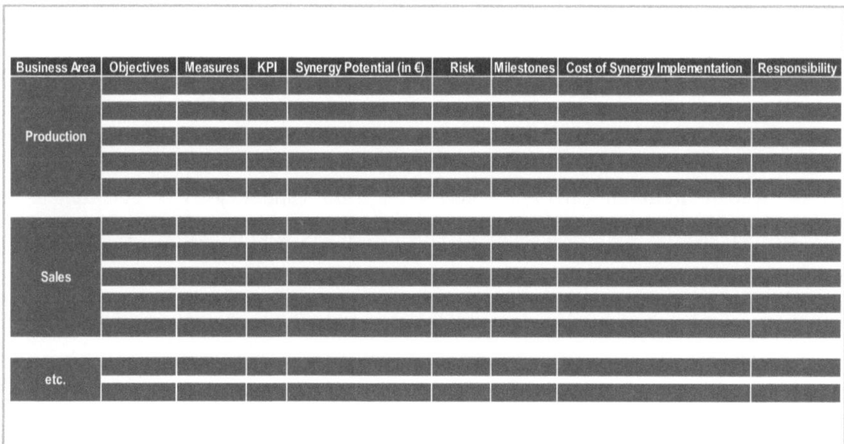

Source: Own illustration based on Lechner 2005, P.16.

Figure 8: Exemplary Draft of an Action Plan for Synergy Tracking

4.2.4 Monitoring and Reporting

A regularly conducted progress review and report of the synergy realization process is a further task of the synergy tracking. The reporting system supports the synergy management with the synergy realization and the prevention of dysergies.[132] Therefore, the synergy track-

[128] See Biberacher 2003, P.485-486.
[129] See Kuster et al. 2008, P.23-24.
[130] See Thomaschewski 2004, P.191-192.
[131] See Lechner; Meyer 2005, P.15.
[132] See Biberacher 2006, P.294; Metz 2002, P.192.

ing needs to conduct variance analysis on a regular basis. Projected values, in particular those defined in the action plan, are compared with the current values at a certain point of time.[133] In case of variances, the synergy tracking has to take steps in terms of adjustment measures, which can be imposed to the employees in charge.[134]

This ensures a target-oriented synergy management and secures that the realization process complies with the schedule. In order to provide the synergy management with updated information, the synergy tracking has to operate a permanent monitoring of the ongoing synergy relevant projects and to supply consistent reports at any time.[135] Therefore, it is required to create project specific reports so that every effect can be assigned to their respective project.[136] At the same time, the synergy tracking has to keep the process assessable by the management requiring a comprehensive overview and preventing information gaps. Hence, it is necessary to provide the synergy management with transferable reports.[137]

Furthermore, synergies should be reported on an appropriate level of detail to avoid an information overflow of the synergy management. For this reason, it is advised to identify so-called Key Performance Indicators (KPI), which are important operative financial figures that reflect synergy effects by changing their values.[138] Nevertheless, an ex-post control of synergy effects raises often allocation problems for the synergy tracking. During the synergy realization process there are often synergy effects whose origin cannot easily be determined. For example, an increase of revenues because of new customers who could be acquired under a normal market development would be an example by which KPI would be affected. However, this would not be a result of the M&A transaction and should not be interpreted as a synergy effect. Therefore, the synergy tracking also need to be aware of those general business effects and should encounter these problems by careful analysis of synergy effects.[139]

Due to the complexity of synergy tracking caused by the number of factors that influence the realization process, the Synergy Scorecard, an instrument in accordance with Kaplan and Norton's Balanced Scored, is increasingly used.[140] The Synergy Scorecard connects performance control of financial figures with action control while it combines the synergy goals, expressed through their impact on financial figures, with their respective actions.[141] As a result, complex cause-effect relations and their influence on financial figures can be revealed.

---

[133] See Lechner; Meyer 2005, P.17; Chapter 6.4.
[134] See Biberacher 2003, P.351.
[135] See Lechner Meyer 2003, P.17.
[136] See Weber; Roventa 2006, P.284.
[137] See Lechner; Meyer 2005, P. 17-18; Weber; Roventa 2006, P.284.
[138] See Biberacher 2006, P.294.
[139] See Beck 2003, P.682.
[140] See Kaplan; Norton 1996; Wala 2008, P.30-32; Eckhoff 2006, P.237-238, Biberacher 2006, P.294-296.
[141] See Biberacher 2006, P.294.

4.4 Challenges for Synergy Tracking during Mergers & Acquisitions

The main task of the synergy tracking during the PMI is to support the synergy management effectively. This means, it has to secure the realization of synergy potentials that were identified before the closing of the transaction to pay off the price premium. An increase of the company value is only achieved when synergy effects exceed the amount of synergies that was calculated in the deal value.

According to analysis of M&A transactions by Köppen, the realization time of synergies and the price premium paid on top of the Stand-alone value of the acquisition target are the two factors that influence the probability of synergy realization the most.[142] The longer the realization of synergies is deferred, the lower the probability is to realize those synergies to the projected extent. As mentioned earlier, the dynamic business environment, which can influence projected synergies over time, as well as the impact through the time value of money are the main factors for this effect.[143] Therefore, Eckhoff recommends conducting a comprehensive market-and company analysis ahead of the planning of synergies in order to counter these synergy realization risks.[144]

However, synergy tracking often lacks a sufficient information basis despite the DD when it is expected to plan synergies and identify dysergies. Often the vendor is not willing to disclose all information and enable the acquirer to conduct an in-depth company analysis until the final contracts are signed.[145] One reason for this behavior is that the vendor intends to prevent the usage of information, obtained during the DD, in support of industrial espionage when the buying interest is just pretended in order to gain confidential information about competitors.[146]

Moreover, the assessment of the quality of information that is provided by the target company is difficult to estimate. In order to get the highest possible price, the target company often tends to provide the acquirer with value appreciating company information and limits information that could negatively affect the final company value. Hence, the acquirer cannot always rely on the DD as an information source especially when the vendor tries to provide incomplete or manipulated information.[147] As a result, the acquirer might pay an unjustified acquisition price for the target company due to lack of information prior to the transaction, which increases the risk to fail the realization of the desired synergies and cause value destruction.

---

[142] See Köppen 2004, P.49-58.
[143] See Chapter 4.2.3; Chapter 5.2.
[144] See Eckhoff 2006, P.87-89.
[145] See Gildemeister 2008, P.37.
[146] See Nölting 1998, P.122.
[147] See Köppen 2004, P.99.

4.5 Risk Factor Human Capital in Mergers & Acquisitions

M&A provide synergy potentials when job positions can be optimized and redundant work can be abolished. Therefore, M&A transactions are regularly burdening the workforce psychologically. Layoffs within M&A transactions can be expected. This can lead to a huge insecurity among the workforce and affect the entire M&A process negatively.[148] In particular, employees who work for administrative departments in which often jobs are consolidated are likely to be concerned. For instance, people who work in finance and controlling departments who conduct synergy tracking and are expected to show high performance during M&A are directly affected.[149] Therefore, it is suggested to communicate the company`s proposals openly and make integrations measures transparent, comprehensible and justifiable for the employees. This company approach prevents insecurity of employees and averts rumors among the workforce about possible developments within the company. However, the moment of sharing this information and the decision of the person that should be entitled to communicate, have to be thoughtfully planned.[150]

Another issue relating human capital during M&A transactions appears because of motivational aspects. M&A transactions are events that include a high degree of complexity which results in a demanding workload for the people involved. Moreover, it is often experienced that after an M&A transaction synergy efforts are neglected right after the officially closing of the deal. Employees continue with daily business and are not concerned with the past M&A project anymore. [151] This is why the synergy tracking should integrate an incentive system that motivates employees to contribute to the synergy realization targets. The incentive system has to incorporate financial benefits, such as performance-based bonuses as well as Non financial benefits like personal development prospects. In addition, the synergy management has to connect the incentives with the required measures to achieve the synergy goals. As a result, the incentive system supports a goal-driven conduction of the synergy realization process and ensures a commitment to the objectives among the employees.[152]

Beyond motivational issues, the management often has to deal with different corporate cultures of the involved organizations. The organizational as well as operational structure often varies between the merging businesses. Thus, internal processes are handled differently and responsibilities are assigned to people working at different hierarchical levels. These "culture clashes" occasionally result in employee resistance when employees become unmotivated and

[148] See Gerds; Schewe 2009, P.98-107.
[149] See Weber; Roventa 2006, P.282-283.
[150] See Unger 2007, P.890-891; Weber; Roventa 2005, P.281-283.
[151] See Lechner; Meyer 2005, P.14.
[152] See Ibid., P.16; Biberacher 2003, P.511-522.

refuse to adapt to new corporate cultures.[153] Therefore, it is often required to apply methods of change management in order to reconcile the business cultures.[154]

4.6 Institutional Integration of Synergy Tracking

The tasks of synergy tracking can generally be assigned to the financial controlling department of an organization, which facilitates the coordination between synergy tracking and financial controlling on the strategic as well as organizational level. However, a risk of this is that the complex task of synergy tracking is seen as an exotic function within the department and tends to be neglected. Because of that, it is crucial to assign specific responsibilities for synergy tracking on the top level of the controlling department. It makes sure that synergy-related aspects are recognized as an important task of the controlling department and employees feel committed to conduct them appropriately.[155]

Since synergy tracking is not only to be conducted on the top level, but also in the specific functional departments at the operational level, Biberacher suggests to establish a central synergy tracking department on the top level and to assign further responsibilities to employees in charge of the functional departments.[156] A different approach suggests Thomaschewski who recommends assembling an interdisciplinary acquisition team that is supported by experts from the functional departments on a case by case basis. On the other hand Eckhoff opts to integrate synergy tracking on a high organizational level, such as the investment controlling department underlining the main goal of an organization, increasing the company value, and emphasizing the synergy tracking's importance to achieve this goal.[157]

Conclusively it can be said that there is no overall solution as to how synergy tracking has to be incorporated into an organization.

A variety of factors exist that determine the success of the institutional integration of synergy management. Therefore, this decision should be made depending on the specific case.

[153] See Larsson 2004, P.9-11.
[154] See Unger 2007, P.891-893.
[155] See Biberacher 2003, P.524.
[156] See Biberacher 2003, P.526.
[157] See Thomaschewski 2004, P.196; Eckhoff 2006, P.79-83.

5 Valuation of Synergy Potentials in Mergers & Acquisitions

5.1 Company Valuation as a Framework for Synergy Valuation

In M&A transactions, the company value of the target company has to be differentiated between objective and the subjective company value. The objective company value is determined by the value of the target company in case the company would be run as it did before without merging with another company. This value does not include any possible impacts the potential acquirer or other prospective buyers might have on the company value (Stand-alone value).[158] The relevant value drivers are the projected future cash flows obtained through operative business activities on stand-alone basis and other cash in- and outflows that, for instance, occur resulting from investments forecasted in the single business plan. The subjective company value on the other hand includes all positive and negative effects such as synergies, dysergies and integration costs, which emerge in case of an M&A transaction.[159]

The actual synergy value can be calculated by two different approaches, the synoptic approach and the incremental approach. The synoptic approach is applied by subtracting the Stand-alone values of the respective companies from the combined company value. In this case, the synergy value results in the remaining sum of the subtraction. The incremental approach on the other hand is characterized through synergy effects which are calculated in a separate financial statement and subsequently added to the single business plans. This approach is adopted in most scientific literature, since it provides a more detailed overview of synergy effects and facilitates synergy tracking during the PMI.[160]

A variety of company valuation methods exist, which serve as important instruments in many business cases and provide their users with solutions for various topics of business. Particularly in M&A transaction, these valuation methods are fundamental for the calculation of acquisition targets. Moreover, company valuation methods are applied in order to value synergy potentials that result from M&A transactions. As mentioned above, the DCF analysis, as the most used company valuation method within M&A, is applied in order to present the synergy valuation procedure. The DCF analysis is considered to be the most suitable valuation method for synergy valuation. This is because it can incorporate the most influential factors, such as the forward-looking focus, periodic forecast, time value of money, and consideration of risk. Therefore, it provides a high level of flexibility in its application.[161] Another reason for its popularity is due to the widely recognized shareholder value principle. M&A transactions are

[158] See Lucks; Meckl 2002, P.176.
[159] See Coenenberg; Jakoby 2000, P.191-198.
[160] See Köppen 2004, P.117-124; Lechner; Meyer 2003, P.368-369.
[161] See Biberacher 2003, P.436-438.

increasingly seen as a special form of investment. According to the shareholder value principle, the maximization of shareholder value is the main goal by making financial decisions. The DCF analysis, in which future cash flows are discounted in order to determine the investment success, is the most recognized method in this context since it provides sufficient results to make investment decisions.[162]

5.2 Discounted Cash Flow Analysis

5.2.1 Fundamentals

The DCF analysis is based on projected future cash flows which are discounted by a risk-adjusted interest rate in order to calculate the Present Value (PV) of a cash flow stream. Due to the discount effect, cash flows in more distant future contribute less to the accumulated PV of the cash flow stream so that the time value of money principle is taken into account. Except for financial synergies that can impact on the discount rate, most synergies can be numerically expressed in changes of cash flows. Therefore, the DCF analysis supports synergy tracking as a sophisticated calculation scheme. An in-depth cash flow analysis, as part of the DCF analysis, is required to plan synergies in detail and enables to trace cash flow changes back to the operational level where the synergy effect was realized. Furthermore, the DCF analysis works in planning synergies over time as a result of its periodic structure.[163] The DCF systematic for company valuation is illustrated in the figure below (See Figure 9):

[162] See Thomaschewski 2004, P.88.
[163] See Biberacher 2003, P.439.

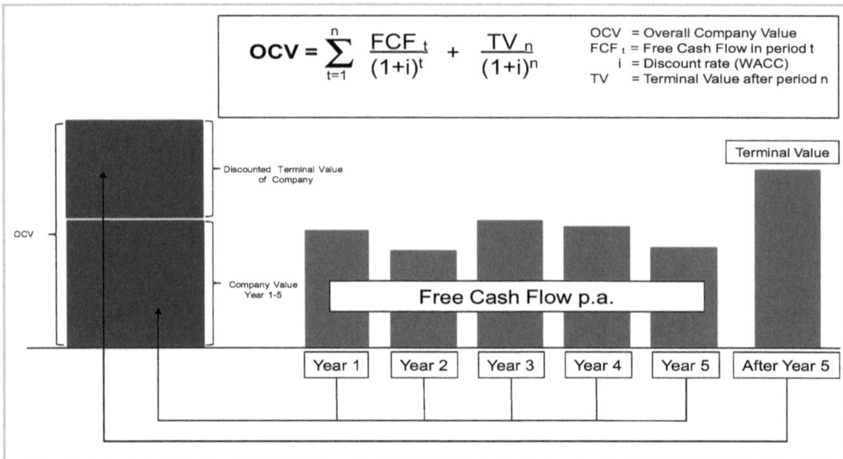

Source: Own illustration based on Lucks; Meckl 2002, P.180-181.

Figure 9: Calculation Scheme of DCF Analysis for Company Valuation

There are different approaches in which the DCF concept is applied. In this context, the entity- and equity-approach are the most used in practice. These approaches differ relating their input and their focus on the capital structure. The entity-approach is based on the cash flow before financial expenditure, such as interest expenses which are then discounted by the Weighted Average Cost of Capital (WACC). In contrast, the equity-approach uses the cash flow after interests and taxes, and discounts only the equity holders` cost of capital after tax.[164] However, the approaches lead to the same result when both calculations were done under the same assumptions.[165] Since the applied discount rate (WACC) has to correspond with the cash flow-values, the entity-approach is applied in the following.

5.2.2 Periodic Net-Synergy Cash Flows

In order to work out the synergy value of an M&A transaction with the DCF analysis, synergy-induced free cash flows have to be calculated. Based on the forecasted balanced sheets and the income statements of both companies on stand-alone basis and the forecasts of the combined financial statements including synergies and integration costs, synergy-induced free cash flows can be calculated. To make synergy tracking possible, the action plan which includes all measures to be taken to create the projected synergies need to be used simultane-

[164] See Thomaschewski 2004, P.55-59.
[165] See Coenenberg; Jakoby 2000, P.193.

ously.[166] While profit increasing synergies affect the synergy cash flow directly, cost synergies cannot be quantified until a comparison between the single and combine income statements was made.[167] To make reliable forecasts of synergy-induced free cash flows a period of 5 years should not be exceeded.[168] The following figure gives an overview of the calculation procedure of net-synergy cash flows (See Figure 10):

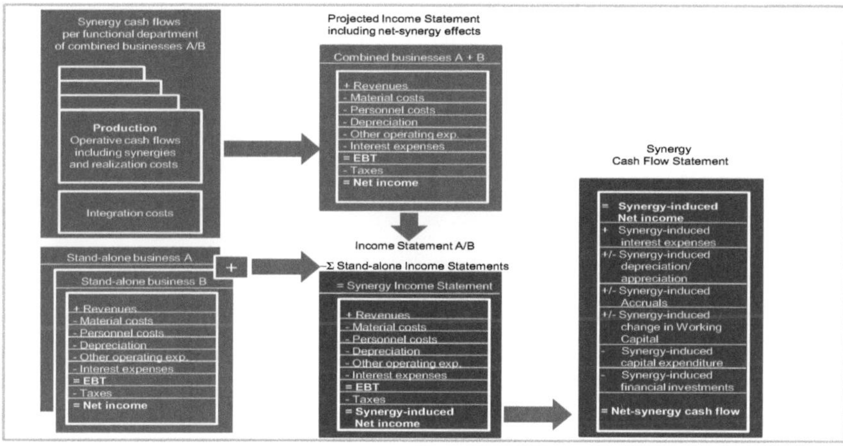

Source: Own illustration based on Eckhoff 2006, P.193.

Figure 10: Calculation of Net-Synergy Cash Flows with the Indirect Method

Apart from the indirect method free cash flows can also be calculated based on the direct method. Hereby free cash flows are calculated by deducting all cash outflows from cash inflows. However, a detailed forecast of all cash-related business transactions is often difficult to forecast.[169] As in figure 9 shown, a terminal value (TV) of the company is part of the calculation. This value reflects the company value for the years after the detailed planning period. The cash flows, that determine the TV, are often projected with a constant growth rate into perpetuity. It is assumed that the company will not be liquidated in the future but continues to operate for an unforeseeable amount of time (going concern principle).[170] Synergies, however, should not be calculated in these cash flows because they cannot be considered as perpetual and should therefore only be part of cash flows in the detail planning period.[171]

---

[166] See Köppen 2004, P.119.
[167] See Eckhoff 2006, P.193.
[168] See Biberacher 2003, P.142; Coenenberg; Jakoby 2000, P.192.
[169] See Perridon; Steiner 1999, P.590-591; Thomaschewski 2004, P.50; Biberacher 2003, P.135-136.
[170] See Wirtz 2003, P.221.
[171] See Eckhoff 2006, P.194.

5.2.3 Calculation of Discount Rates for Synergy Valuation

The discount rate that is used in the DCF analysis for company valuation depends on the chosen DCF method. As mentioned before, the following synergies are valued using the entity approach in order to consider their comprehensive impact on a company. The entity approach takes the WACC as the discount rate, which is calculated as follows:

$$WACC = \frac{E}{V} \times i_{equity} + \frac{D}{V} \times i_{debt} (1 - T_c)$$ [172]

Where:

i_{equity} = *cost of equity*

i_{debt} = *cost of debt*

E = *market value of the firm`s equity*

D = *market value of the firm`s debt*

V = *volume (E + D)*

T_c = *corporate tax rate*

As can be seen, the WACC equation includes the cost of each capital component multiplied by its proportional weight. The tax deductable interest expenses on debt are taken into account by lowering the cost of debt. Accordingly, the calculation is based on cash flows before interest expenses in order to avoid double consideration of the interest tax shield.[173] The cost of debt depends on the realization risk of the synergy cash flows estimated by the capital lenders. If lenders presume that the synergy-induced cash flows will not be generated as initially expected, a higher interest rate on financing will be demanded and will lead to a higher cost of debt. This effect could be countered by financial synergies, which result in lower interest rates on financing charged by banks due to a higher credit rating after the merger. In order to apply a synergy specific cost of debt rate the entire financing volume ought to be meant exclusively to generate the synergy-related cash flows.[174] This is often difficult to determine. Therefore, a common average cost of debt rate is applied in the following calculations. A more complicated approach is required in order to determine the cost of equity included in the denominator of the WACC equation. A forecast of the rate of return demanded by shareholders depends on external factors, such as forecasts of the future economic development, political decisions, and the financial situation of the company. These factors have to be considered to measure the risk of the investment for a shareholder. Hence, they have to be analyzed specifically for the

[172] See Wirtz 2003, P. 217.
[173] See Wirtz 2003, P.217.
[174] See Eckhoff 2006, P.195.

synergy-induced free cash flows in order to get a synergy specific return on equity.[175] To simplify this process the Capital Asset Pricing Model (CAPM) is often applied to calculate the cost of equity, which is defined as follows:

$$i_{equity} = r_f + \beta\,(r_m - r_f)^{176}$$

Where:

r_f = *risk free rate*

β = *beta factor*

r_m = *expected market return*

The CAPM can be divided into two components. The first component is indicated as the risk free rate which is the rate of return obtained by an investor if he invested his money in the capital market with a minimum of risk. Therefore, returns of short-term treasury bonds, which assumingly involve the lowest risk among securities on the capital market, are often applied. The second component is obtained by multiplying the difference between the market return, which is derived from the market portfolio, and the risk free rate by the beta factor. This difference is called the risk premium and reflects the rate demanded by an investor if he invested in the company to cover the company specific risk. The beta factor is a statistical sensitivity measurement, which reflects the volatility between the market portfolio and the share price of the respective company. By adding both components together the cost of equity, which is the rate of return based on the risk involved in investing in the respective company demanded by the shareholders, can be computed.[177]

5.2.4 Assessment of Discounted Cash Flow Analysis

Although the DCF analysis is often criticized because of assumptions, such as an efficient capital market and the existence of a market portfolio, it is the most applied method in practice among various company valuation methods.[178] In particular the comparison between an investment in a financial security and a shareholder`s investment in a company has become increasingly recognized (Shareholder-value principle) over the last years. Regarding the synergy valuation the DCF is advantageous since it provides the option to plan synergies in detail and valuate them separately by discounting the respective synergy-related cash flows. This supports particularly the synergy management process during the PMI when synergy tracking

---

[175] See Ibid., P.196-197.
[176] See Gallati 2003, P.311-313.
[177] See Wirtz 2003, P.218; Perridon; Steiner 1999, P.497-502.
[178] See Picot 2008, P.390; Lucks; Meckl 2002, P.182.

is of great importance. In addition, the DCF enables to calculate an accumulated synergy value for company valuation.[179]

5.3 Consideration of Synergy Realization Probabilities

As mentioned before, synergies are always projected under uncertainty. The synergy management does not know if the planned synergies will finally be realized. Therefore, probabilities which ease the influence of uncertainty by impacting on synergy values are used by making forecasts. There are different approaches to include probabilities in the synergy valuation process. Bruner suggests the application of different discount rates while valuing synergy effects based on their risk of realization.[180] Biberacher mentions the scenario technique as possible alternative in which future forecasts for synergy effects are made under different assumptions in order to come to an expected synergy value which derives from the outcomes of the different scenarios.[181] Another approach uses weighted synergy-induced cash flows based on their realization probability. For example cost reduction synergies as a result of a decrease of overhead costs as a "most likely synergy" may get weighted by 100%, whereby revenue increasing synergies, such as cross-selling effects, are more uncertain and are only weighted by 70%, accordingly.[182]

[179] See Thomaschewski 2004, P.86-92.
[180] See Bruner 2004, P.332-334.
[181] See Biberacher 2003, P.130-133.
[182] See Wöginger 2006, P.212.

6 Synergy Tracking Tool for Post Merger Integration

6.1 Introduction

In this chapter a possible tracking tool for the PMI of an M&A transaction is presented. Based on the requirements on synergy tracking mentioned in the two previous chapters, this tool serves as a tracking instrument and supports the synergy tracking and the synergy management during the synergy realization process. However, it is not claimed to be a universal tracking tool, which can be applied in every M&A transaction in its current version, but it highlights the general functions and components that are required to track synergies during the PMI.

The tracking tool is based on internal cost calculation frameworks of each of the involved businesses and tracks synergies by analyzing variances between the single business plan and the merged business plan. The final synergy value is obtained by applying the DCF analysis with the indirect method. It should be mentioned that there are also tracking techniques that are predominately build on cash flow statements and that use cost calculation as a supplement.[183] However; an extension of the tracking tool in this concern is possible.

The following part of this chapter gives an overview of the structure describing the main components of the tracking tool. Subsequently, connections between synergy-related measures within an organization and their effects on synergy values are made. Moreover, the variance analysis, as an important task of the synergy tracking, as well as additional functions of the tracking tool to provide the synergy management with information during the PMI, is described. Finally, an application example is presented in order to highlight the systematization of the tracking tool.

6.2 Structure

6.2.1 Single Business Plan

The first components of the synergy tracking tool are the single business plans of the respective companies on stand-alone basis. These business plans are created in pre-merger phases based on information obtained during the Due Diligence and own business forecasts for the acquiring company. In order to cater for a realistic level of detail, cost calculations for both businesses are forecasted for the planning period 1-5. An extended planning period is not recommended because of external factors that influence synergies over time so that a reliable forecast beyond this period is unlikely and increases the risk of overestimating synergy poten-

[183] See Biberacher 2003, P.134-144, 354-369.

tials. The forecasted financial figures in the cost calculations provide the data for the income statements of each company. Both income statements are later added together and result in the combined income statement. This income statement presents the combined financial forecast for both companies assuming that each business would continue to operate as a separate entity. It also sets the threshold which has to be exceeded in order to achieve synergy potentials in an M&A transaction.

6.2.2 Synergy Action Plan

The synergy action plan is the second component of the tracking tool. This plan consists of a detailed list of planned measures that need to be taken after the merger process in order to realize synergy potentials. Also dysergies, integration costs and other associated costs caused by synergy measures are integrated.

Furthermore, each action is connected to a financial figure on which the synergy effect impacts and becomes visible in its numerical extent (Key Performance Indicator). In addition, responsibilities are assigned to the respective employees in charge (KPI holder). Despite cases in which several KPI holders are appointed due to cross-functional synergies, a clear assignment of responsibilities has to be remained in order to ensure a successful synergy tracking.

All synergies are tracked regarding their time of occurrence and their duration of impact. The time of occurrence and the duration of synergies should correspond to the respective project plans of each single measure and should be used as a guideline during the project execution. The impact of probabilities should be incorporated by conducting scenario analysis or weighted synergy values in order to come to a realistic estimation of synergy potentials before the closing of the M&A transaction. However, this tracking tool is mainly for synergy tracking during the PMI, and hence does not include probability calculations.

In addition, the planned synergies expressed in financial figures over the planning period are part of the action plan. These synergy values can be used as a demand on the employees, which need to fulfill the task, and can support a self-control system at the operational level.

6.2.3 Merged Business Plan

After synergy potentials are identified and included in the synergy action plan, the projected financial figures for the merged business can be transferred in the synergy tracking tool. The merged business plan provides the platform to integrate all figures that were forecasted including synergies, dysergies. and integration costs. This plan consists of three different tracking instruments that are described in the following. Each projected financial figure can be included in the cost calculation spreadsheet of the merged business plan. In order to remain a comprehensive overview, the tool is limited on selected direct costs that can be directly allocated to their respective departments. The tracking tool does also provide the option to extend the cost calculation and to apply internal cost allocation techniques to tackle also overhead costs. The projected figures for the merged business are automatically transferred to the variance analysis tool which allocates the costs to their respective departments. In this tool, the projected figures are compared to the current figures that are obtained in the PMI (variance analysis). In addition, the budget figures are transferred to the merged income statement which incorporates all expenditure and revenues including synergies and integration costs of the business after the M&A transaction.

6.2.4 Synergy Business Plan

After the combined income statement and the merged income statement were planned, the synergy business plan can be created. As the difference of both income statements, the synergy income statement is generated by subtracting the combined income statement from the merged counterpart. This results in an income statement which extracts precisely the synergy values in each position of the net income calculation. In order to calculate the synergy value over the planning period, net-synergy cash flows are calculated by applying the indirect cash flow method. Based on the net-synergy cash flows an accumulated synergy value over the planning period can be calculated. These synergy values are part of the reporting sheet to provide the management with the necessary information about the synergy values over the planning period in an aggregated form.

6.3 Allocation of Synergy Effects

In the synergy income statement, synergy effects can be tracked directly. Revenue enhancing synergies, for instance, attained through cross-selling synergies become transparent by increased synergy –induced sales revenue. In case of a higher level of complexity due to several synergy effects influencing the revenues, this position has to be subdivided. Categories, such as product, region or place of production, are often chosen to obtain a higher level of detail and to allocate synergy-induced revenues to their origins.[184]

Synergy-induced expenses are expressed as negative numbers on the synergy income statement and lead to an increase of the synergy-induced net income. In order to determine responsibilities for certain synergies, the synergy action plan delivers the required information.

[184] See Biberacher 2003, P.138-139.

6.4 Variance Analysis

During the PMI, the synergy tracking has to provide the synergy management with information in support of making decisions to realize the projected synergy effects. In order to track variations of current figures from budget figures, a variance analysis has to be constantly conducted. In case of negative or positive deviations from the projected value, the variance analysis tool highlights the place of occurrence and indicates the extent of the deviation. Accordingly, variances can be identified and reported to the synergy management that is then able to make adjustments. In addition, reasons, which led to the deviation, can be analyzed by using the tracking tool and demanding reports from the people in charge of the respective synergy measure (KPI holder). Apart from the variance analysis tool, variance analyses are conducted in the synergy income statement and the reporting sheet. The reporting sheet provides instantly the synergy management with an overview of the current development of the synergy values so that reports to the top level management can be delivered at every stage of the PMI.

6.5 Application Example: NewCo

The financial figures over the planning period 1-5 for the acquiring company NewCo on stand-alone basis were forecasted as follows:

Income Statement NewCO					
Planning Period 1-5 (Figures in million €)					
Financial Items	1	2	3	4	5
Sales Revenue (5% growth p.a.)	50.00	52.50	55.13	57.88	60.78
± Increase/Decrease in finished Goods/Inventory	0.00	0.00	0.00	0.00	0.00
- Material Expenses	10.00	10.00	10.00	10.00	10.00
- Personnel Costs					
- Wages and Salaries*	4.20	4.20	4.20	4.20	4.20
- Turnover/Dism.-Costs	0.00	0.00	0.00	0.00	0.00
- Pension Reserve (50% of Wages/Sal.)	2.10	2.10	2.10	2.10	2.10
- Misc. Personnel Costs (40% of Wages/Sal.)	1.68	1.68	1.68	1.68	1.68
- Depreciation/Amortization (5% p.a.)	5.00	4.75	4.51	4.29	4.07
- Other Operating Expenses**	7.00	7.00	7.00	7.00	7.00
Operting Income	20.02	22.77	25.63	28.61	31.72
± Income/Loss from Investment Activity	0.00	0.00	0.00	0.00	0.00
Net Income from Continuing Operations (EBIT)	20.02	22.77	25.63	28.61	31.72
- Interest Expenses	0.00	0.00	0.00	0.00	0.00
+ Interest Income	0.00	0.00	0.00	0.00	0.00
EBT	20.02	22.77	25.63	28.61	31.72
- Extraordinary Expenses	0.00	0.00	0.00	0.00	0.00
+ Extraordinary Income	0.00	0.00	0.00	0.00	0.00
- Tax Expenses	0.00	0.00	0.00	0.00	0.00
Net Income	20.02	22.77	25.63	28.61	31.72
***Workforce:** **Procurement 30 x 0.03€ , Prod.40 x 0.03€, Sales & Marketing 30 x 0.035€, Admin.30 x 0.035€**					
**** Storage expenses 1.00, Market research 2.00, Advertising 3.00, Other Costs 1.00**					

Source: Own illustration based on Synergy Tracking Tool / Single Business Plan / Income Statement NewCo.

Figure 11: Tracking Tool: Single Business Plan/Income Statement NewCo

In order to increase its market share and catch up with its competitors NewCo`s management has decided to merge with Company B whose financial forecast for period 1-5 on stand-alone basis was as follows:

Income Statement Company B					
Planning Period 1-5 (Figures in million €)					
Financial Items	1	2	3	4	5
Sales Revenue (5% growth p.a.)	20.00	21.00	22.05	23.15	24.31
± Increase/Decrease in finished Goods/Inventory	0.00	0.00	0.00	0.00	0.00
- Material Expenses	5.00	5.00	5.00	5.00	5.00
- Personnel Costs					
- Wages and Salaries*	2.10	2.10	2.10	2.10	2.10
- Turnover/Dism.-Costs	0.00	0.00	0.00	0.00	0.00
- Pension Reserve (50% of Wages/Sal.)	1.05	1.05	1.05	1.05	1.05
- Misc. Personnel Costs (40% of Wages/Sal.)	0.84	0.84	0.84	0.84	0.84
- Depreciation/Amortization (5% p.a.)	2.00	1.90	1.81	1.71	1.63
- Other Operating Expenses**	4.00	4.00	4.00	4.00	4.00
Operting Income	5.01	6.11	7.26	8.45	9.69
± Income/Loss from Investment Activity	0.00	0.00	0.00	0.00	0.00
Net Income from Continuing Operations (EBIT)	5.01	6.11	7.26	8.45	9.69
- Interest Expenses	0.00	0.00	0.00	0.00	0.00
+ Interest Income	0.00	0.00	0.00	0.00	0.00
EBT	5.01	6.11	7.26	8.45	9.69
- Extraordinary Expenses	0.00	0.00	0.00	0.00	0.00
+ Extraordinary Income	0.00	0.00	0.00	0.00	0.00
- Tax Expenses	0.00	0.00	0.00	0.00	0.00
Net Income	5.01	6.11	7.26	8.45	9.69
***Workforce:** **Procurement 15 x 0.03€ , Prod.20 x 0.03€, Sales & Marketing 15 x 0.035€, Admin.15 x 0.035€**					
**** Storage expenses 0.50, Market research 1.00, Advertising 2.00, Other Costs 0.50**					

Source: Own illustration based on Synergy Tracking Tool / Single Business Plan / Income Statement Comapny B.

Figure 12: Tracking Tool: Single Business Plan/Income Statement Company B

As a consequence, the combined income statement of both companies based on the previous financial forecasts has been projected as shown below:

Income Statement Company NewCo + B					
Planning Period 1-5					
(Figures in million €)					
Financial Items	1	2	3	4	5
Sales Revenue	70.00	73.50	77.18	81.03	85.09
± Increase/Decrease in finished Goods/Inventory	0.00	0.00	0.00	0.00	0.00
- Material Expenses	15.00	15.00	15.00	15.00	15.00
- Personnel Costs					
- Wages and Salaries	6.30	6.30	6.30	6.30	6.30
- Turnover/Dism.-Costs	0.00	0.00	0.00	0.00	0.00
- Pension Reserve	3.15	3.15	3.15	3.15	3.15
- Misc. Personnel Costs	2.52	2.52	2.52	2.52	2.52
- Depreciation/Amortization	7.00	6.65	6.32	6.00	5.70
- Other Operating Expenses	11.00	11.00	11.00	11.00	11.00
Operting Income	25.03	28.88	32.89	37.06	41.41
± Income/Loss from Investment Activity	0.00	0.00	0.00	0.00	0.00
Net Income from Continuing Operations (EBIT)	25.03	28.88	32.89	37.06	41.41
- Interest Expenses	0.00	0.00	0.00	0.00	0.00
+ Interest Income	0.00	0.00	0.00	0.00	0.00
EBT	25.03	28.88	32.89	37.06	41.41
- Extraordinary Expenses	0.00	0.00	0.00	0.00	0.00
+ Extraordinary Income	0.00	0.00	0.00	0.00	0.00
- Tax Expenses	0.00	0.00	0.00	0.00	0.00
Net Income	25.03	28.88	32.89	37.06	41.41

Source: Own illustration based on Synergy Tracking Tool / Single Business Plan / Combined Income Statement.

Figure 13: Tracking Tool: Single Business Plan/Combined Income Statement

After analyzing Company B during the Due Diligence, the management of NewCo identified different cost synergy potentials. However, also integration costs were expected to be incurred due to compensation payments paid to employees. Every synergy measure planned ahead of the transaction was recorded in the synergy action plan which is illustrated below:

Synergy-Action Plan								
Functional Department	KPI holder	Measures plannend	Synergy Potential	Synergy Driver	Key Performance Indicator (KPI)	Projected Dysergies/ Integration Costs	Time of Occurence	Duration
Procurement	Head of Department	Negotiations with suppliers about volume discounts	Improved purchase conditions	Lower Purchase Prices	Material Costs*		1	1-5
Shared Services/ Administration	Head of Department/ HR Manager	Consolidation of 10 job positions in administration department over the next 3 Periods after the merger**	Reduction of redundant work positions	Decrease of Personnel Costs	Wages / Salaries, Misc. Personnel Costs, Pension Reserve (In Shared Services / Administration Department)		1	1-5
	Head of Department/ HR Manager	Consolidation of 10 job positions in administration department over the next 3 Periods after the merger			Turnover/Dism.-Costs	Compensation payment***	1	1-3
Sales & Marketing	Manager Market Research	Combining of Market Research Instruments	Process optimization in Market Research	Decrese of Market Research Costs	Market Research (Other Operating Expenses)****		2	2-5
Projected synergy values: *2.00 per period; **Planned layoffs: Period 1: 4, Period 2: 3, Period3: 3; ***Compensation payment: 0.50 per employee; ****1.00 from period 2 on								

Source: Own illustration based on Synergy Tracking Tool / Synergy Action Plan.

Figure 14: Tracking Tool: Synergy Action Plan

The projected synergy values resulting from the measures to be taken in the respective departments over the planning period 1-5 are shown in the synergy income statement below:

Synergy Income Statement NewCO / Company B						
Planning Period 1-5 (Figures in million €)						
Financial Items	1	2	3	4	5	Sum
	projected	projected	projected	projected	projected	projected
Sales Revenue	0.00	0.00	0.00	0.00	0.00	0.00
± Increase/Decrease in finished Goods/Inventory	0.00	0.00	0.00	0.00	0.00	0.00
- Material Expenses	-2.00	-2.00	-2.00	-2.00	-2.00	-10.00
- Personnel Costs						
- Wages and Salaries	-0.14	-0.24	-0.35	-0.35	-0.35	-1.44
- Turnover/Dism.-Costs	0.20	0.15	0.15	0.00	0.00	0.50
- Pension Reserve	-0.07	-0.12	-0.18	-0.18	-0.18	-0.72
- Misc. Personnel Costs	-0.06	-0.10	-0.14	-0.14	-0.14	-0.57
- Depreciation/Amortization	0.00	0.00	0.00	0.00	0.00	0.00
- Other Operating Expenses	0.00	-1.00	-1.00	-1.00	-1.00	-4.00
Synergy-induced Operting Income	2.07	3.32	3.51	3.66	3.66	16.23
± Income/Loss from Investment Activity	0.00	0.00	0.00	0.00	0.00	0.00
Synergy-induced Net Income from Continuing Operations (EBIT)	2.07	3.32	3.51	3.66	3.66	16.23
- Interest Expenses	0.00	0.00	0.00	0.00	0.00	0.00
+ Interest Income	0.00	0.00	0.00	0.00	0.00	0.00
EBT	2.07	3.32	3.51	3.66	3.66	16.23
- Extraordinary Expenses	0.00	0.00	0.00	0.00	0.00	0.00
+ Extraordinary Income	0.00	0.00	0.00	0.00	0.00	0.00
- Tax Expenses	0.00	0.00	0.00	0.00	0.00	0.00
Synergy-induced Net Income	2.07	3.32	3.51	3.66	3.66	16.23

Source: Own illustration based on Synergy Tracking Tool / Synergy Income Statement.

Figure 15: Tracking Tool: Synergy Business Plan/Income Statement

However, the planned job cuts within period 2 could not have been enforced as previously expected due to unexpected strikes led by the trade union. In order to achieve the projected synergy value despite the difficulties in period 2, two additional job cuts over the following periods (3+4) were executed.

Shared Services / Administration:																	
Planning Period 1-5	1		Variance	2		Variance	3		Variance	4		Variance	5		Variance	Sum		Variance
Cost Overview	actual	projected	Analysis	actual	projected	Analysis	actual	projected	Analysis	actual	projected	Analysis	actual	projected	Analysis	actual	projected	Analysis
Personnel Costs:																		
Wages and Salaries	1.44	1.44	0.00	1.40	1.33	0.07	1.23	1.23	0.00	1.16	1.23	-0.07	1.16	1.23	-0.07	6.37	6.44	-0.07
Turnover/Dism.-Costs	0.20	0.20	0.00	0.05	0.15	-0.10	0.25	0.15	0.10	0.10	0.00	0.10	0.00	0.00	0.00	0.60	0.50	0.10
Pension Reserve	0.72	0.72	0.00	0.70	0.67	0.04	0.61	0.61	0.00	0.58	0.61	-0.04	0.58	0.61	-0.04	3.19	3.22	-0.03
Misc. Personnel Costs	0.57	0.57	0.00	0.56	0.53	0.03	0.49	0.49	0.00	0.46	0.49	-0.03	0.46	0.49	-0.03	2.55	2.58	-0.03
Accumulated Personnel Costs	2.93	2.93	0.00	2.71	2.68	0.03	2.58	2.48	0.10	2.29	2.33	-0.03	2.19	2.33	-0.13	12.70	12.74	-0.03

Negative variance from projected personnel costs after period 2 due to failed layoff enforcement

Adjustments through two additional layoffs in period 3 and 4

Accumulated positive variance from projected personnel costs after period 1-5

Source: Own illustration based on Synergy Tracking Tool / Variance Analysis Tool.

Figure 16: Tracking Tool: Variance Analysis/Shared Services/Administration

In addition, the synergy management, while analyzing the reporting sheet, had to decide that planned cost cuts in market research activities in period 2 could not have been achieved as initially calculated. Consequently, the management demanded reports from the responsible manager at the market research department (KPI holder). The management was told that unforeseeable integration difficulties occurred right after the departments merged and processes had to be reconciled. Fortunately, research costs could be cut by 200.000 € in each of the following periods because of well-conducted implementation projects after period 2 market.
The developments caused by the adjustments over the planning period are illustrated in the extract of the variance analysis tool below:

Sales & Marketing:																		
Planning Period 1-5	1		Variance	2		Variance	3		Variance	4		Variance	5		Variance	Sum		Variance
Cost Overview	actual	projected	Analysis	actual	projected	Analysis	actual	projected	Analysis	actual	projected	Analysis	actual	projected	Analysis	actual	projected	Analysis
Market Research	3.00	3.00	0.00	2.20	2.00	0.20	1.80	2.00	-0.20	1.80	2.00	-0.20	1.80	2.00	-0.20	10.60	11.00	-0.40

Integration problems in period 2

Process optimization in the following periods 3 - 5

Accumulated positive variance from projected market research costs after period 1-5

Source: Own illustration based on Synergy Tracking Tool / Variance Analysis Tool.

Figure 17: Tracking Tool: Variance Analysis/Sales & Marketing

The reporting sheet of the synergy tracking tool provides the synergy management with the following financial figures relating the development of the net-synergy cash flows as well as the accumulated synergy values over the planning period compared to the projected figures:

Calculation of Synergy Values / Variance Analysis

DCF Analysis (Entity Approach)												
Planning Period 1-5												
(Figures in million €)												
WACC :	10%											
	1		2		3		4		5		Sum	
	actual	projected	actual	projected	actual	projected	actual	projected	actual	projected	actual	projected
Net-Synergy Cash Flow per period =	2.14	2.14	3.17	3.44	3.79	3.69	4.11	3.84	4.21	3.84	17.41	16.94
Variance from projected Net-Synergy Value	0.00		-0.27		0.10		0.27		0.37		0.47	
Synergy Value over time =	1.94	1.94	4.56	4.78	7.41	7.56	10.21	10.18	12.83	12.56		
Variance from projected Synergy Value	0.00		-0.22		-0.15		0.04		0.27			

Actual PV of Net-Synergy Cash Flow stream at the beginning of period 1

Exceeding amount of the Net-Synergy Cash Flow stream over the planning period (WACC 10%)

Projected PV of Net-Synergy Cash Flow stream at the beginning of period 1

Source: Own illustration based on Synergy Tracking Tool / Reporting Sheet.

Figure 18: Tracking Tool: Reporting Sheet

7 Summary and Future Perspectives

The majority of M&A transactions are still pursued as a consequence of forecasted synergy potentials. However, the past has shown that in many cases previously identified synergy potentials have not been realized when businesses have continued to operate after the merger. There has been an unexpected difference between identified synergy potentials and synergies which were actually realized during the PMI.

Reasons, such as inaccessible information during the Due Diligence, an overestimation of synergy potentials and an unawareness of dysergies and integration costs before the merger, have often been mentioned by managements. Moreover, synergies have been often assumed as continual effects without considering external factors by which every business is affected. Due to a constantly increasing pace in the business sector, an ever rising competition on several markets along with a shortening of product lifecycles, synergies nowadays, whose existence could be formerly presumed as long-lasting, need to be analyzed carefully regarding their duration.

As a result excessive price premiums have been paid which could not have been compensated by synergy effects after the M&A transactions.[185]

Therefore, it is inevitable to analyze acquisition targets thoroughly and make realistic assumptions concerning synergy potentials. Furthermore, an effective synergy tracking as support function of the synergy management has to be implemented particularly in the actively acquiring businesses. It has to gather, to process, and to provide required information by the synergy management over the entire M&A process. This implies that synergy management and synergy tracking have to set in during pre-merger phases so that it takes part while synergy potentials are identified and is able to intervene when acquisition targets tend to be excessively evaluated. This provides the synergy management with a comprehensive overview of the M&A transaction, which contributes to a continuous integration of this important institution and avoids possible interface problems during the M&A process.

During the last two years it could be determined that particularly M&A transactions as a motive for highly-yielded investment opportunities, predominately conducted by financial investors, experienced a declining trend. This was caused by credit constraints due to reserved bank lending activity. However, after a massive drop of business transactions on the M&A market during the financial crisis in 2008 and its aftermath, which brought the M&A market to its lowest point in the second quarter of 2009, M&A activity has been recovered since then. It is supposed, that particularly large businesses with sufficient equity resources will be increas-

[185] See Köppen 2004, P.132.

ingly acquisitive in order to take advantage of the large number of undervalued businesses currently available on the M&A market. Furthermore, companies will be stronger concentrated on their core business which will lead to strategically driven spin-offs and other forms of demerger. In addition, the M&A market will be influenced by business insolvencies and restructuring cases as a result of the hardship that many businesses experienced during the financial crisis so that an increasing number of M&A transactions can be expected in the future.[186]

Conclusively it can be said, that M&A transactions constitute a promising strategic opportunity for businesses if their positive effects, such as synergies, can offset negative effects, such as integration costs, risk of complexity, and cultural tensions. Moreover, external growth through M&A has to be analyzed and compared with organic growth achieved by internal business development to decide whether M&A presents the best alternative.

[186] See Deloitte 2010, P.2-7.

Bibliography

Al-Ani, A.; Rettberg, B.; Humburg, S. (2005): Der Erfolg von Zusammenschlüssen darf kein Zufall sein: Ein Synergiecontrolling macht Vorteile von Fusionen sichtbar, In: Betriebswirtschaftliche Blätter, No.4, P.194-200.

Ansoff, H. I. (1965): Corporate Strategy: An analytic approach to business policy for growth and expansion, New York.

A.T. Kearney (2002/2003): Global PMI Study.

Beck, R. (2003): Synergie-Controlling als Weg aus der „Synergiefalle"?, In: Controlling, 15th Vol., No.12, P.675-682.

Biberacher, J. (2003): Synergiemanagement und Synergiecontrolling, Munich.

Biberacher, J. (2006): Synergiecontrolling - Bindeglied zwischen Akquisitionszielen und Realisierung, In: Controlling & Management, 50th Vol., No.5, P.291-297.

Bire, A. (2009): Synergiemanagement im Rahmen von Mergers & Acquisitions: Eine zentrale Herausforderung für das Pre-Merger Controlling, Available on: http://www.controllingportal.de/upload/old/pdf/fachartikel/funktionsspezifisch/ADCURAM_Synergiemanagement_MA_20091203_final.pdf, last access: 20.06.2010.

Borowicz, F. et al. (2006): Strategisches Management von Mergers & Acquisitions: State of the Art in Deutschland und Österreich, Wiesbaden.

Booz Allen & Hamilton (2001): Merger Integration: Delivering on the Promise, McLean, Virgina.

Bragg, S. M. (2008): Mergers & Acquisitions: A Condensed Practitioner's Guide, Hoboken, N.J.

Bruner, R. F. (2004): Applied Mergers and Acquisitions, Hoboken, N.J.

Coenenberg, A. G.; Jakoby, S. (2000): Akquisition und Unternehmensbewertung, In: Busse von Colbe, W. et al. (eds.): Betriebswirtschaft für Führungskräfte, 30th Vol., Stuttgart.

Damodaran, A. (2005): The Value of Synergy, Available on: http://pages.stern.nyu.edu/~adamodar/pdfiles/papers/synergy.pdf, last access: 20.06.2010.

Deimel, K.; Isemann; R.; Müller, S. (2006): Kosten- und Erlösrechnung: Grundlagen, Managementaspekte und Integrationsmöglichkeiten der IFRS, Munich.

Deloitte (2009): Post Merger Integration: Akquisitionen erfolgreich integrieren: Was Top-Performer besser machen, Dusseldorf.

Deloitte (2010): M&A-forum: Chancen und Risiken für M&A, Dusseldorf.

DePamphilis, D. M. (2009): Merger, acquisitions, and other restructuring activities, 5th ed., Oxford.

Eckhoff, J. (2006): Synergiecontrolling im Rahmen von Mergers & Acquisitions, In: Möller, H. P.; Peemöller, V. H.; Richter, M. (eds.): Schriftenreihe zum Finanz-, Prüfungs- und Rechnungswesen, 42nd Vol., Munich.

Fischer, L. J. (2008): Wertorientiertes Kundenmanagement bei M&A Transaktionen, Lohmar.

Gallati, R. R. (2003): Risk Management and Capital Adequacy, New York.

Gerds, J. (2000): Post Merger Integartion: Eine empirische Untersuchung zum Integrationsmanagement, Wiesbaden.

Gerds, J.; Schewe G. (2009): Post Merger Integration: Unternehmenserfolg durch Integration Excellence, 3rd, updated and extended ed., Berlin.

Gildemeister, A. (2008): Synergiebewertung: Identifikation und Quantifizierung von Synergien im M&A-Kontext, Norderstedt.

Goold, M.; Campbell, A. (1998): Desperately seeking synergy, In: Harvard Business Review, 76th Vol. No.5, P.130-143.

Jansen, S. A. (2001): Mergers & Acquisitions: Unternehmensakquisitionen und-kooperationen, 4th, updated and extended ed., Wiesbaden.

Kaplan, R. S.; Norton, D. P. (1996): The Balanced Scorecard: Translating Strategy into Action, Boston.

Kerler, P. (1999): Mergers & Acquisitions und Shareholder Value, Zurich.

Kuster, J. et al. (2008): Handbuch Projektmanagement, 2nd, updated ed., Berlin.

Larsson, R. et al. (2004): The Secrets of Merger and Acquisition Success: A Co-Competence and Motivational Approach to Synergy Realization, In: Pablo, A. L.; Javidan, M. (eds.): Mergers and Acquisitions: Creating Integrative Knowledge, Oxford.

Larsson, R. (2005): Synergy Realization in Mergers & Acquisitions: A Co-Competence and Motivational Approach, In: Stahl, K. G.; Mendenhall, M. E. (eds.): Mergers and Acquisitions: Managing Culture and Human Resources, Stanford.

Lechner, H.; Meyer, A. (2003): Quantifizierung von Synergiepotentialen bei Unternehmenszusammenschlüssen, In: M&A Review, 13th Vol., No.8/9, P.367-372.

Lechner, H.; Meyer, A. (2005): Vom Potential zum Effekt – Integriertes und strukturiertes Synergiemanagement, In: M&A Review, 15th Vol., No.1, P.13-19.

Lucks, K.; Meckl, R. (2002): Internationale Mergers & Acquisitions: Der prozessorientierte Ansatz, Berlin.

Metz, M. (2002): Controlling des Integrationsprozesses bei Mergers & Acquisitions, In: Kahle, E. (eds.): Entscheidungs-und Organisationstheorie, Wiesbaden.

Nölting, A. (1998): Nabelschau: Due Diligence, In: Manager Magazin, 28th Vol., No.10, P.120-130.

Paprottka, S. (1996): Unternehmenszusammenschlüsse: Synergiepotentiale und ihre Umsetzungsmöglichkeiten durch Integration, In: Jacob, H. (eds.): Betriebswirtschaftliche Forschung zur Unternehmensführung, 30th Vol., Wiesbaden.

Perridon, L.; Steiner, M. (1999): Finanzwirtschaft der Unternehmung, 10th, updated ed., Munich.

Picot, G. (2008): Handbuch Mergers & Acquisitions: Planung-Durchführung-Integration, 4th, fundamentally revised and updated ed., Stuttgart.

Porter, M. E. (1999): Wettbewerbsvorteile: Spitzenleistung erreichen und behaupten, 5th ed., Frankfurt/New York.

Reinke, B. (1996): Synergiemanagement im Handel, In: Ahlert, D. (eds.): Schriften zu Distribution und Handel, 21st Vol., Frankfurt.

Sodeik, N. (2009): Projektmanagement wertorientierter Mergers & Acquisitions, In: Szyperski, N. et al. (eds.): Planung, Organisation und Unternehmensführung, 124th Vol., Lohmar.

Thomaschewski, D. (2004): Synergien im Akquisitionsmanagement, Lohmar.

Unger, M. (2007): Post Merger Integration, In: Polster-Grüll, B.; Zöchling, H.; Kranebitter, G. (eds.): Handbuch Mergers & Acquisitions: Rechtliche und steuerliche Optimierung: Ausgewählte Fragen der Bewertung und Finanzierung, Vienna.

Wala, T. (2008): Synergiecontrolling: Bewertung und Controlling von Synergien im Rahmen von M&A-Transaktionen, Saarbrücken.

Weber, J.; Roventa P. (2006): Synergiemanagement und Synergiecontrolling bei M&A-Projekten, In: Controlling & Management, 50th Vol., No.5, P.280-285.

Wirtz, B. W. (2003): Mergers & Acquisitions Management: Strategie und Organisation von Unternehmenszusammenschlüssen, Wiesbaden.

Wöginger, H. (2006): Das Synergy-Value-Konzept – ein ganzheitlicher Ansatz zur Synergieevaluation bei Mergers & Acquisitions, In: M&A Review, 16th Vol., No.5, P.205-213.

Appendix

Synergy Tracking Tool: Single Business Plan/Income Statement Company A:

Income Statement Company A					
Planning Period 1-5 (Figures in million €)					
Financial Items	1	2	3	4	5
Sales Revenue	0.00	0.00	0.00	0.00	0.00
± Increase/Decrease in finished Goods/Inventory	0.00	0.00	0.00	0.00	0.00
- Material Expenses	0.00	0.00	0.00	0.00	0.00
- Personnel Costs					
- Wages and Salaries	0.00	0.00	0.00	0.00	0.00
- Turnover/Dism.-Costs	0.00	0.00	0.00	0.00	0.00
- Pension Reserve	0.00	0.00	0.00	0.00	0.00
- Misc. Personnel Costs	0.00	0.00	0.00	0.00	0.00
- Depreciation/Amortization	0.00	0.00	0.00	0.00	0.00
- Other Operating Expenses	0.00	0.00	0.00	0.00	0.00
Operting Income	0.00	0.00	0.00	0.00	0.00
± Income/Loss from Investment Activity	0.00	0.00	0.00	0.00	0.00
Net Income from Continuing Operations (EBIT)	0.00	0.00	0.00	0.00	0.00
- Interest Expenses	0.00	0.00	0.00	0.00	0.00
+ Interest Income	0.00	0.00	0.00	0.00	0.00
EBT	0.00	0.00	0.00	0.00	0.00
- Extraordinary Expenses	0.00	0.00	0.00	0.00	0.00
+ Extraordinary Income	0.00	0.00	0.00	0.00	0.00
- Tax Expenses	0.00	0.00	0.00	0.00	0.00
Net Income	0.00	0.00	0.00	0.00	0.00

Synergy Tracking Tool: Single Business Plan/Income Statement Company B:

Income Statement Company B					
Planning Period 1-5					
(Figures in million €)					
Financial Items	1	2	3	4	5
Sales Revenue (5% growth p.a.)	0.00	0.00	0.00	0.00	0.00
± Increase/Decrease in finished Goods/Inventory	0.00	0.00	0.00	0.00	0.00
- Material Expenses	0.00	0.00	0.00	0.00	0.00
- Personnel Costs					
- Wages and Salaries	0.00	0.00	0.00	0.00	0.00
- Turnover/Dism.-Costs	0.00	0.00	0.00	0.00	0.00
- Pension Reserve	0.00	0.00	0.00	0.00	0.00
- Misc. Personnel Costs	0.00	0.00	0.00	0.00	0.00
- Depreciation/Amortization (5% p.a.)	0.00	0.00	0.00	0.00	0.00
- Other Operating Expenses	0.00	0.00	0.00	0.00	0.00
Operting Income	0.00	0.00	0.00	0.00	0.00
± Income/Loss from Investment Activity	0.00	0.00	0.00	0.00	0.00
Net Income from Continuing Operations (EBIT)	0.00	0.00	0.00	0.00	0.00
- Interest Expenses	0.00	0.00	0.00	0.00	0.00
+ Interest Income	0.00	0.00	0.00	0.00	0.00
EBT	0.00	0.00	0.00	0.00	0.00
- Extraordinary Expenses	0.00	0.00	0.00	0.00	0.00
+ Extraordinary Income	0.00	0.00	0.00	0.00	0.00
- Tax Expenses	0.00	0.00	0.00	0.00	0.00
Net Income	0.00	0.00	0.00	0.00	0.00

Synergy Tracking Tool: Single Business Plan/Combined Income Statement:

Income Statement Company A + B					
Planning Period 1-5					
(Figures in million €)					
Financial Items	1	2	3	4	5
Sales Revenue	0.00	0.00	0.00	0.00	0.00
± Increase/Decrease in finished Goods/Inventory	0.00	0.00	0.00	0.00	0.00
- Material Expenses	0.00	0.00	0.00	0.00	0.00
- Personnel Costs					
- Wages and Salaries	0.00	0.00	0.00	0.00	0.00
- Turnover/Dism.-Costs	0.00	0.00	0.00	0.00	0.00
- Pension Reserve	0.00	0.00	0.00	0.00	0.00
- Misc. Personnel Costs	0.00	0.00	0.00	0.00	0.00
- Depreciation/Amortization	0.00	0.00	0.00	0.00	0.00
- Other Operating Expenses	0.00	0.00	0.00	0.00	0.00
Operting Income	0.00	0.00	0.00	0.00	0.00
± Income/Loss from Investment Activity	0.00	0.00	0.00	0.00	0.00
Net Income from Continuing Operations (EBIT)	0.00	0.00	0.00	0.00	0.00
- Interest Expenses	0.00	0.00	0.00	0.00	0.00
+ Interest Income	0.00	0.00	0.00	0.00	0.00
EBT	0.00	0.00	0.00	0.00	0.00
- Extraordinary Expenses	0.00	0.00	0.00	0.00	0.00
+ Extraordinary Income	0.00	0.00	0.00	0.00	0.00
- Tax Expenses	0.00	0.00	0.00	0.00	0.00
Net Income	0.00	0.00	0.00	0.00	0.00

Synergy Tracking Tool: Synergy Action Plan:

Synergy-Action Plan													
Functional Department	KPI holder	Measures plannend	Synergy Potential	Synergy Driver	Key Performance Indicator (KPI)	Projected Dysergies/ Integration Costs	Time of Occurence	Duration	Synergy effect per period Figures in (million €)				
									1	2	3	4	5
									0.00	0.00	0.00	0.00	0.00

Synergy Tracking Tool: Merged Business Plan/Merged Income Statement:

Income Statement Company A/B																		
Planning Period 1-5																		
(Figures in million €)																		
Financial Items	1		Variance	2		Variance	3		Variance	4		Variance	5		Variance	Sum		Variance
	current	projected	Analysis	current	projected	Analysis	current	projected	Analysis	current	projected	Analysis	current	projected	Analysis	current	projected	Analysis
Sales Revenue	0.00	0.00	0.00	0.00	0.00	0.00	0.00	0.00	0.00	0.00	0.00	0.00	0.00	0.00	0.00	0.00	0.00	0.00
± Increase/Decrease in finished Goods/Inventory	0.00	0.00	0.00	0.00	0.00	0.00	0.00	0.00	0.00	0.00	0.00	0.00	0.00	0.00	0.00	0.00	0.00	0.00
- Material Expenses	0.00	0.00	0.00	0.00	0.00	0.00	0.00	0.00	0.00	0.00	0.00	0.00	0.00	0.00	0.00	0.00	0.00	0.00
- Personnel Costs																		
- Wages and Salaries	0.00	0.00	0.00	0.00	0.00	0.00	0.00	0.00	0.00	0.00	0.00	0.00	0.00	0.00	0.00	0.00	0.00	0.00
- Turnover/Dism.-Costs	0.00	0.00	0.00	0.00	0.00	0.00	0.00	0.00	0.00	0.00	0.00	0.00	0.00	0.00	0.00	0.00	0.00	0.00
- Pension Reserve	0.00	0.00	0.00	0.00	0.00	0.00	0.00	0.00	0.00	0.00	0.00	0.00	0.00	0.00	0.00	0.00	0.00	0.00
- Misc. Personnel Costs	0.00	0.00	0.00	0.00	0.00	0.00	0.00	0.00	0.00	0.00	0.00	0.00	0.00	0.00	0.00	0.00	0.00	0.00
- Depreciation/Amortization	0.00	0.00	0.00	0.00	0.00	0.00	0.00	0.00	0.00	0.00	0.00	0.00	0.00	0.00	0.00	0.00	0.00	0.00
- Other Operating Expenses	0.00	0.00	0.00	0.00	0.00	0.00	0.00	0.00	0.00	0.00	0.00	0.00	0.00	0.00	0.00	0.00	0.00	0.00
Operting Income	0.00	0.00	0.00	0.00	0.00	0.00	0.00	0.00	0.00	0.00	0.00	0.00	0.00	0.00	0.00	0.00	0.00	0.00
± Income/Loss from Investment Activity	0.00	0.00	0.00	0.00	0.00	0.00	0.00	0.00	0.00	0.00	0.00	0.00	0.00	0.00	0.00	0.00	0.00	0.00
Net Income from Continuing Operations (EBIT)	0.00	0.00	0.00	0.00	0.00	0.00	0.00	0.00	0.00	0.00	0.00	0.00	0.00	0.00	0.00	0.00	0.00	0.00
- Interest Expenses	0.00	0.00	0.00	0.00	0.00	0.00	0.00	0.00	0.00	0.00	0.00	0.00	0.00	0.00	0.00	0.00	0.00	0.00
+ Interest Income	0.00	0.00	0.00	0.00	0.00	0.00	0.00	0.00	0.00	0.00	0.00	0.00	0.00	0.00	0.00	0.00	0.00	0.00
EBT	0.00	0.00	0.00	0.00	0.00	0.00	0.00	0.00	0.00	0.00	0.00	0.00	0.00	0.00	0.00	0.00	0.00	0.00
- Extraordinary Expenses	0.00	0.00	0.00	0.00	0.00	0.00	0.00	0.00	0.00	0.00	0.00	0.00	0.00	0.00	0.00	0.00	0.00	0.00
+ Extraordinary Income	0.00	0.00	0.00	0.00	0.00	0.00	0.00	0.00	0.00	0.00	0.00	0.00	0.00	0.00	0.00	0.00	0.00	0.00
- Tax Expenses	0.00	0.00	0.00	0.00	0.00	0.00	0.00	0.00	0.00	0.00	0.00	0.00	0.00	0.00	0.00	0.00	0.00	0.00
Net Income	0.00	0.00	0.00	0.00	0.00	0.00	0.00	0.00	0.00	0.00	0.00	0.00	0.00	0.00	0.00	0.00	0.00	0.00

Synergy Tracking Tool: Synergy Business Plan/Income Statement:

Synergy Income Statement Company A/B																		
Planning Period 1-5																		
(Figures in million €)																		
Financial Items	1		Variance	2		Variance	3		Variance	4		Variance	5		Variance	Sum		Variance
	current	projected	Analysis	current	projected	Analysis	current	projected	Analysis	current	projected	Analysis	current	projected	Analysis	current	projected	Analysis
Sales Revenue	0.00	0.00	0.00	0.00	0.00	0.00	0.00	0.00	0.00	0.00	0.00	0.00	0.00	0.00	0.00	0.00	0.00	0.00
± Increase/Decrease in finished Goods/Inventory	0.00	0.00	0.00	0.00	0.00	0.00	0.00	0.00	0.00	0.00	0.00	0.00	0.00	0.00	0.00	0.00	0.00	0.00
- Material Expenses	0.00	0.00	0.00	0.00	0.00	0.00	0.00	0.00	0.00	0.00	0.00	0.00	0.00	0.00	0.00	0.00	0.00	0.00
- Personnel Costs																		
- Wages and Salaries	0.00	0.00	0.00	0.00	0.00	0.00	0.00	0.00	0.00	0.00	0.00	0.00	0.00	0.00	0.00	0.00	0.00	0.00
- Turnover/Dism.-Costs	0.00	0.00	0.00	0.00	0.00	0.00	0.00	0.00	0.00	0.00	0.00	0.00	0.00	0.00	0.00	0.00	0.00	0.00
- Pension Reserve	0.00	0.00	0.00	0.00	0.00	0.00	0.00	0.00	0.00	0.00	0.00	0.00	0.00	0.00	0.00	0.00	0.00	0.00
- Misc. Personnel Costs	0.00	0.00	0.00	0.00	0.00	0.00	0.00	0.00	0.00	0.00	0.00	0.00	0.00	0.00	0.00	0.00	0.00	0.00
- Depreciation/Amortization	0.00	0.00	0.00	0.00	0.00	0.00	0.00	0.00	0.00	0.00	0.00	0.00	0.00	0.00	0.00	0.00	0.00	0.00
- Other Operating Expenses	0.00	0.00	0.00	0.00	0.00	0.00	0.00	0.00	0.00	0.00	0.00	0.00	0.00	0.00	0.00	0.00	0.00	0.00
Synergy-induced Operting Income	0.00	0.00	0.00	0.00	0.00	0.00	0.00	0.00	0.00	0.00	0.00	0.00	0.00	0.00	0.00	0.00	0.00	0.00
± Income/Loss from Investment Activity	0.00	0.00	0.00	0.00	0.00	0.00	0.00	0.00	0.00	0.00	0.00	0.00	0.00	0.00	0.00	0.00	0.00	0.00
Synergy-induced Net Income from Continuing Operations (EBIT)	0.00	0.00	0.00	0.00	0.00	0.00	0.00	0.00	0.00	0.00	0.00	0.00	0.00	0.00	0.00	0.00	0.00	0.00
- Interest Expenses	0.00	0.00	0.00	0.00	0.00	0.00	0.00	0.00	0.00	0.00	0.00	0.00	0.00	0.00	0.00	0.00	0.00	0.00
+ Interest Income	0.00	0.00	0.00	0.00	0.00	0.00	0.00	0.00	0.00	0.00	0.00	0.00	0.00	0.00	0.00	0.00	0.00	0.00
EBT	0.00	0.00	0.00	0.00	0.00	0.00	0.00	0.00	0.00	0.00	0.00	0.00	0.00	0.00	0.00	0.00	0.00	0.00
- Extraordinary Expenses	0.00	0.00	0.00	0.00	0.00	0.00	0.00	0.00	0.00	0.00	0.00	0.00	0.00	0.00	0.00	0.00	0.00	0.00
+ Extraordinary Income	0.00	0.00	0.00	0.00	0.00	0.00	0.00	0.00	0.00	0.00	0.00	0.00	0.00	0.00	0.00	0.00	0.00	0.00
- Tax Expenses	0.00	0.00	0.00	0.00	0.00	0.00	0.00	0.00	0.00	0.00	0.00	0.00	0.00	0.00	0.00	0.00	0.00	0.00
Synergy-induced Net Income	0.00	0.00	0.00	0.00	0.00	0.00	0.00	0.00	0.00	0.00	0.00	0.00	0.00	0.00	0.00	0.00	0.00	0.00

Synergy Tracking Tool: Synergy Business Plan/Cash Flow Statement:

Synergy Cash Flow Statement

Indirect Method

Planning Period 1-5

(Figures in million)

Financial Items	1		Variance	2		Variance	3		Variance	4		Variance	5		Variance	Sum		Variance
	current	projected	Analysis	current	projected	Analysis	current	projected	Analysis	current	projected	Analysis	current	projected	Analysis	current	projected	Analysis
Synergy-induced Net Income	0.00	0.00	0.00	0.00	0.00	0.00	0.00	0.00	0.00	0.00	0.00	0.00	0.00	0.00	0.00	0.00	0.00	0.00
+ Synergy-induced Interest Expenses	0.00	0.00	0.00	0.00	0.00	0.00	0.00	0.00	0.00	0.00	0.00	0.00	0.00	0.00	0.00	0.00	0.00	0.00
- Synergy-induced Interest Income	0.00	0.00	0.00	0.00	0.00	0.00	0.00	0.00	0.00	0.00	0.00	0.00	0.00	0.00	0.00	0.00	0.00	0.00
+ Synergy-induced Depreciation/Amortization	0.00	0.00	0.00	0.00	0.00	0.00	0.00	0.00	0.00	0.00	0.00	0.00	0.00	0.00	0.00	0.00	0.00	0.00
+ Pension Reserve	0.00	0.00	0.00	0.00	0.00	0.00	0.00	0.00	0.00	0.00	0.00	0.00	0.00	0.00	0.00	0.00	0.00	0.00
± Change in Working Capital	0.00	0.00	0.00	0.00	0.00	0.00	0.00	0.00	0.00	0.00	0.00	0.00	0.00	0.00	0.00	0.00	0.00	0.00
+ Synergy-induced Capital Expenditure	0.00	0.00	0.00	0.00	0.00	0.00	0.00	0.00	0.00	0.00	0.00	0.00	0.00	0.00	0.00	0.00	0.00	0.00
+ Synergy-induced Financial Investments	0.00	0.00	0.00	0.00	0.00	0.00	0.00	0.00	0.00	0.00	0.00	0.00	0.00	0.00	0.00	0.00	0.00	0.00
Net-Synergy Cash Flow	0.00	0.00	0.00	0.00	0.00	0.00	0.00	0.00	0.00	0.00	0.00	0.00	0.00	0.00	0.00	0.00	0.00	0.00

Synergy Tracking Tool: Reporting Sheet:

Calculation of Synergy Values / Variance Analysis												
DCF Analysis (Entity Approach)												
Planning Period 1-5												
(Figures in million €)												
WACC :	10%											
	1		2		3		4		5		Sum	
	current	projected	current	projected	current	projected	current	projected	current	projected	current	projected
Net-Synergy Cash Flow per period =	0.00	0.00	0.00	0.00	0.00	0.00	0.00	0.00	0.00	0.00	0.00	0.00
Variance from projected Net-Synergy Value	0.00		0.00		0.00		0.00		0.00		0.00	
Synergy Value over time =	0.00	0.00	0.00	0.00	0.00	0.00	0.00	0.00	0.00	0.00		
Variance from projected Synergy Value	0.00		0.00		0.00		0.00		0.00			